NORWAY'S INTERNAL MIGRATION TO NEW FARMS SINCE 1920

EUROPEAN DEMOGRAPHIC MONOGRAPHS

I

Norway's Internal Migration to New Farms since 1920

by

KIRK H. STONE

University of Georgia

MARTINUS NIJHOFF / THE HAGUE / 1971

ISBN 90 247 5130 6

CONTENTS

LIST OF ILLUSTRATIONS

to the Pasvik River (background) and adjoining the one-
north-south local road. About 12 km. (7 1/4 mi.) SW of
Svanvik village on 14 August 1964. 53

Acknowledgments

Sincere gratitude is expressed for financial aid and assistance during field work in Norway during 1955-56, 1958, 1959, 1960, 1964 and 1970 as well as for office support in between. Special appreciation is noted for the following: in the U.S.A. the Geography Branch of the Office of Naval Research in the Department of the Navy, at the University of Georgia the Cartographic Services Laboratory, James R. Carter (research assistant), the Instructional Resources Center, and the Franklin College of Arts and Sciences, at the University of Wisconsin the Graduate School and the University Cartographic Laboratory as well as research assistants Prof. John Tuck, Jr. (University of Georgia), D.R. Every, and Prof. M. H. Aamodt (Brigham Young University), and Editor Wilfred Webster at the American Geographical Society of New York; and in Norway, the office of the U.S. Educational Foundation, Professor Fridtjov Isachsen of the University of Oslo, Dr. A. Løddesøl of of the Norwegian Bog Association, Secretary G.H. Paulsen of *Ny Jord*, Mr. Erling Kristiansen of Bennett's *Reisebureau*, Captain Andreas Rygg of the Royal Norwegian Navy, Secretary Olav Ringstad of the state Agricultural Office, Lektor Ludvig Hertzberg of the University of Oslo; and field assistants Fil. Lic. G.E. Norling (Länsstyrelsen, Stockholm, Sweden) and W.K. Johnson (McGraw Hill Co.), and the literally dozens of gracious Norwegian settlers, local officials, and innkeepers who continuously swamped me with coffee and kindnesses. Mostly I wish to thank the women of my life, Katie, Bun, and Marty, for putting up with it all and always believing in its value.

NORWAY'S INTERNAL MIGRATION TO NEW FARMS SINCE 1920

Norway's internal migration resembles that of many other nations. There are numerous currents, some strong or weak and some paralleling or opposites. The predominant one in this century has been the rural-to-urban movement. But an important counter-current, particularly since 1920, has been that to new farms. Though secondary in numbers to urbanizing and presently of little force, this intra-rural movement of Norwegians has been significant to local and national officials. Further, it might become important again but it certainly includes valuable lessons for planners in all countries.

Geographical changes have resulted from these inner movements. Cities have expanded. Several rural districts have had declines in population. But in still other parts of rural Norway expansions of the inhabited areas have occurred; most of these have been by movements of less than 35 kilometers to areas of new group settling with some kind of state subsidy. It is to these local advances into unsettled land that attention is directed here. The purpose is to outline the bases and geographical extent of a major part of Norway's internal population movement in the past half century and to show planners the problems and results of this action. The technique of analysis is an examination of selected national trends related to rural settling and the study of four sample areas which are representative of these national changes as well as of Norway's great locational differences.

NATIONAL POPULATION CHANGES

Although none of the samples dates from the time of earliest settling in Norway,[1] each is representative of at least one major national change in numbers or location since about 1800. After that the first significant variation was loss of people by emigration. This was of slight importance until 1865 but from then until 1930 emigration was a major element in Norway's population development.[2] In these 65 years 85°/o of the total emigration of about 900,000 people took place; the years of greatest emigration being 1880 through 1883, 1887, and 1888 and 1902 through 1907, when the annual loss was 20,000 to 29,000 persons. The greater losses were from the rural districts, predominantly males who were in farming, fishing, and forestry. The main reason for going was lack of opportunity for profitable employment in Norway, especially in comparison with the United States where most of them went. After 1911 the yearly departures averaged about 8000 to 1930, then declined to a few hundred per year until 1948, and since then have increased to about 2000 persons per annum. The effect on the rural districts was to slow their growth considerably until 1930.

The total population has grown steadily but slowly since 1900, when there were about 2.2 million people in Norway. Since then the average annual growth has averaged about .8%, being just that figure for the years 1958-1969. Meanwhile, another national change was taking place: the more rapid increase of population in the towns and cities. Whereas in 1815 townspeople comprised 9.8% of the total, the number grew slowly to 15.5% in 1865, to 18.3% by 1875, to 23.7% in 1890, to 28% in 1900.[3] Since then, and by a different computation, the urban portion of Norway's population went from 35.7% in 1900 to 50.1% in 1946 to 57.3% in 1960; after 1946 there was an actual decline in numbers of rural people from 1,575,000 to 1,532,000 in 1960.[4]

This urban growth was paralleled by a decline of the birth rate, about which concern was expressed before and after World War II,[5] from 29.8 per 1000 in 1901 to 17.2 per 1000 in 1963. At the same time, the number employed in manufacturing and construction industries increased rapidly to 36% of the economically active population in 1960, while those in agriculture and forestry declined to almost 15%.[6] Thus, rural communities in many parts of Norway have been confronted with accelerated depopulating, primarily of younger people moving to the cities or to industries from farms too small or sites with too high degrees of isolation. The problem is similar to that in Sweden[7] except that Norway's areas of abandoning are small.

Another Norwegian population change took place during World War II. The nation was occupied by the Nazis from 1940 to 1945 and during that period many persons fled or were caused to flee the country. Several cities were damaged severely by bombing. In northern Norway, the greater effect on the rural landscape was the destruction of farm buildings during the 1944 retreat; that change was only temporary for the sites were reoccupied as soon

With the exception of Korea, interestingly enough, there was no tendency for low ICOR countries to have experienced high rates of growth in per capita GNP during the 1960s, most such percentage growth rates being small (e.g., Guatemala, 2.2; Nicaragua, 3.3; Zambia, 2.0; India, 2.6; Malawi, 3.6; Sierra Leone, 2.6; Bolivia, 2.1; El Salvador, 2.2; Thailand, 4.6), relative to that of Korea's (6.8). The explanation for this may consist partly in Korea's more successful population policy. Population growth rates in all of the above low ICOR countries exceeded those in Korea over the 1960-70 period. For such countries it may be that social policy is more or less efficient in terms of capital investment but rather less so with respect to other aspects of growth. The multidimensionality of successful developmental policy is of course well-recognized if not always successfully addressed.

The efficiency of the Korean investment pattern is also confirmed by an examination of the allocation of capital to machinery and equipment, or M and E (48 per cent of gross fixed capital formation for the period 1966-68) relative to other countries.[13] The Korean allocation to M and E approximates, for example, the Latin American average (48.6 per cent) which consists of countries at considerably higher levels of development. Since ICORs in LDCs tend to be lower in the manufacturing sector than for the economy as a whole, capital and labor would appear to be used more efficiently in manufacturing than in other sectors -- a point confirmed by the earlier discussion of the service sector in LDCs. The high Korean growth rate suggests additionally that capital allocated to other activities is more than normally efficient as well, although sectoral ICORs for most LDCs are not available, making international comparisons impossible at this time. Low

ICORs in the private sector are a consequence of the profit maximization goals of firms, while decisions to allocate investment between private and public (infrastructure) sectors are heavily influenced by government. Consequently, both private and public decision-makers in Korea seem clearly to have made relatively efficient use of their capital resources.

Tax Mobilization

The financing of merit, public, and quasi-public goods is a crucial problem for most LDCs. National security, education, public health, law and order, water and sewage, are important, both in their own right and as services to more directly productive activities. So too are roads, ports, dams, communication systems and other necessary features of an infrastructure adequate to assist and sustain growth. Direct government investment in productive activity is also warranted in some circumstances. In some cases, these merit and public goods can wholly or partly be provided by market decision-makers; in others only by government; in still others by some combination of public and private sector involvement. The "appropriate" method of finance for any particular merit or public good is not a settled matter, although very general efficiency guidelines do exist in the normative policy literature.[14] In real circumstances, demands for government financing of goods and services -- arising either out of the not uncommon ideological bias for public sector involvement or, more rationally, an appreciation of efficiency criteria -- are inevitably acute.

From whatever sources demands on the political system are derived, the ability of government to deliver goods and services depends upon its fiscal capacity -- national income and the proportion of national income it can collect in taxes. An inadequate revenue system may, in addition to limiting the supply of public goods, also stimulate inflationary pressure or limit the government's capacity to control such pressure. In LDCs, where development is often contingent on generating exports, inflation can have the devastating consequence, by adding to the demand for imports, of so eroding a country's balance of payments position as to limit or halt growth altogether. Tax capacity is for these reasons a crucial aspect of development.

There is considerable variation among LDCs in the ratio of tax revenue to GDP. The UNCTAD secretariat's study of development effort was able from available data to rank some thirty-six LDCs from a high of 26.6 per cent (Uruguay) to a low of 7.7 per cent (Pakistan) of GDP captured through taxation for the period roughly from 1950-65.[15] Korea, with an average ratio of taxes to GDP of 9.2 per cent for the 1957-64 period, ranked thirty-third in the comparison. Although the UN study is careful to point out that cultural and historical traditions (not to say types of political regimes and calculated efficiency-based decisions) vary greatly across LDCs in influencing the proportions and types of goods and services which will be provided by the private and public sectors, the clear implication is that countries with higher tax/GDP ratios will be better able to assist the developmental process than will other countries.

Surprisingly, however, the UN study does not examine whether countries with higher tax ratios tend to be, as expected, countries with higher growth rates. As noted, average tax ratios for the period 1950-65 (shorter periods were analyzed in some cases) for thirty-six LDCs were developed in the UN study. Since the impact of tax ratios on growth might be expected to be both short and long term, an examination of the relationship between tax ratios and growth rates might include growth rate data for some portion of the period for which tax ratios are compiled, as well as for some period beyond.

If average growth rates in per capita income for the 1960-72 period (meeting the above requirements) are compared for the thirty-six LDCs for which tax ratios were examined by the UN project, it turns out that none of the variation in growth rates is in fact explained by tax ratios (R^2 = .009). High rates of mobilization of the social product through taxation has not, for these LDCs, been associated with growth. Low tax ratios and high growth are just as likely to occur as high tax ratios and low growth. It seems, therefore, that any use of high tax ratios as a developmental measure of effort or performance must be seriously qualified if not disregarded entirely. Public sector use of tax revenues may as easily (perhaps more easily) be inefficient as efficient and as negative as positive in terms of growth. Not only may public sector decision-makers not know how to allocate public revenues to greatest social affect (assuming they have incentive to do so), high tax levels may very well inhibit the propensity of individuals to save, to invest, to take risks, to work, in short, to act developmentally. In any event, the relatively low tax ratio in Korea during 1957-64 (one of the lowest) and its high growth rate during 1960-72 (the highest for countries surveyed) suggests that it is altogether possible that a low tax ratio is consistent with high growth when, as in Korea, other policy decisions combine to encourage developmental behavior.

For example, the income elasticity of government revenue collections to growth in GDP for the 1955-65 period was very high in Korea–(1.8), in fact third out of twenty-two LDCs studied. Income elasticity of tax revenue for the latter

Table 3-5

Rankings of Selected LDCs by Actual Tax/GNP Ratio (1960-65) and Rates of Growth in Per Capita GNP (1960-72)

	Tax Ratio(a)	Rank	Growth in per capita GNP(b)	Rank
Uruguay	26.6	1	-0.1	35
Israel	26.0	2	5.7	3
Zambia	22.9	3	2.0	26
Brazil	22.3	4	3.2	9
Tunisia	21.9	5	3.1	12
Chile	20.8	6	2.1	23
Malaysia	18.5	7	3.1	13
Mauritius	17.6	8	- 0.2	36
Argentina	17.4	9	2.7	16
Guyana	17.1	10	1.4	31
Kenya	16.6	11	3.6	6
Venezuela	16.5	12	1.8	28
Barbados	16.0	13	3.2	8
Peru	15.8	14	2.2	22
Ecuador	15.3	15	2.3	18
Burma	15.1	16	0.8	33
Jamaica	14.9	17	3.1	11
Taiwan	14.5	18	6.8	2
Costa Rica	14.2	19	3.1	10
Uganda	13.9	20	2.2	21
Panama	13.4	21	4.5	5
S. Vietnam	12.8	22	0.8	34
India	12.5	23	1.1	32
Sierra Leone	12.3	24	2.6	17
Trinidad and Tobango	12.3	25	2.8	15
Bolivia	11.8	26	2.1	24
Tanzania	11.8	27	2.9	14
Philippines	10.7	28	2.2	19
Colombia	10.7	29	1.8	27
Thailand	10.2	30	4.6	4
Honduras	10.1	31	1.5	30
Nigeria	10.1	32	2.0	25
KOREA	9.2	33	6.8	1
Paraguay	8.9	34	1.5	29
Guatemala	8.7	35	2.2	20
Pakistan	7.7	36	3.3	7

Coefficient of correlation (r) between (a) and (b) = .095.

SOURCE: Tax data from UNCTAD, *The Measurement of Development Effort* (New York, 1970), p. 29; income data from *World Bank Atlas*, 1974.

half of that period (1960-65), however, fell sharply to .62 (for every 1 per cent increase in GDP, tax revenues grew at .62 per cent), which was relatively very *low* (thirtieth out of thirty-three LDCs analyzed).[16] The sharp rise and then fall in income elasticity for tax revenue was of course accompanied by high growth rates in both periods. Whether those elasticities were a conscious contrivance of growth-oriented decision-makers is not clear, although they were by all accounts not inconsistent with growth. By 1970, tax revenue was 14 per cent of GDP, where it roughly remained throughout the early 1970s.[17] These proportions will rise in the late 1970s with the introduction of value added taxation. Taxes will by 1978 capture 18-19 per cent of GNP, allowing for an enlargement in the supply of public goods and social welfare. Stability in tax burdens has its benefits: (1) government planners can anticipate and make incremental improvements in meritorious and tested programs without the decision burdens and risks inherent in dispensing disproportionately expanding revenues to less than first priority demands, and (2) individuals can calculate their own allocative problems more competently when their tax burden is more or less constant and predictable. Of course, stability in tax/GDP ratios, while an important goal, should properly follow the establishment of the "right" social balance, and what the size of the public sector "should" be relative to the private sector is not a matter that will yield to any precise rule.

At the very least, however, it may be said that the typical bias among LDCs for large relative expansions in the public sector often lacks reasonable justification and may well be self-defeating not only with respect to growth but to equity as well. It must also be noted in this connection that taxation is not the only source of government revenue in

Korea or in any other country and that any preferred social balance must take these into account: receipts from government services, loan repayments, income from public enterprises, borrowings, counter-part funds (no longer available in Korea), and so forth. These additional sources of revenue can be very significant. For example, 1974 tax revenues in Korea were only 42 per cent of total revenue. On this basis, total projected government revenues were 30 per cent of GNP. The largest sources of non-tax revenue were the state communications and railroad monopolies. As already mentioned, these and other enterprises have adopted opportunity cost pricing policies for the most part and, consequently, have not themselves limited the government in performing its indispensable role as a provider of public goods and services.

Export Performance

Korean growth has been export-led and policy-makers have sought, generally successfully, to stimulate and assist this development. The importance of exports in economic development is manifest: a vigorous export sector provokes domestic growth, expedites specialization and provides the foreign exchange necessary to meet import requirements for improved consumer choice, technology and primary materials. When exports involve primary products, the familiar problems of market instability and limited demand often ensue, two important reasons for the efforts among many LDCs to diversify their exports. Diversification in most circumstances is possible only by adding value by manufacturing finished or more highly finished products. Growth in manufactured exports, by making more efficient use of domestic resources, also stimulates domestic demand and makes feasible the economic establishment of import-substituting industries.

Libya (a petroleum exporter) excepted, Korea ranked as the fastest growing LDC in the world over the 1955-65 period in terms of rate of growth in exports. From 1960-65, Korean average annual export growth was a phenomenal 34.3 per cent. This was a substantially higher growth rate than other fast-growing LDC exporters experienced for the same period (e.g., Panama, 22.7 per cent; Taiwan 22.4 per cent; Nicaragua, 20.2 per cent and Jordan, 17.5 per cent) and was far in excess of the LDC median (N = 57) of 8.1 per cent.[18] The expansion of Korean exports has persisted: in 1960 exported goods and services were valued at less than $40 million, in 1970 at $1.4 billion, and in 1976 at $7.8 billion. For the period 1970-74, exports grew by 228 per cent or 45.6 per cent annually. The rate of growth for 1974 was a slower but still very high 39 per cent, a level still insufficient to compensate for the 63 per cent growth in imports, most of which was due to the much higher costs of raw materials.[19]

For 1975, a bleak year internationally for all exporters (oil producers excepted), and a severe testing time for resource-poor industrializing countries, Korea still managed a 17 per cent growth in exports and growth in real GNP of 7.5 per cent, a reassuring achievement in view of the turn down in the economies of Korea's chief trading partners, the United States and Japan.[20]

Deterioration in the terms of trade during 1973-75 was reflected in the $5.9 billion in short and long term debt accumulated by the end of 1975, up 34 per cent from 1974 (some of which was used earlier to finance internal development but, more recently, largely for debt service). External debt will continue to increase in the future and the capacity to manage that debt soundly, although not now seriously questioned, could deteriorate if exports are not increased apace. For 1976, GNP rose 15 per cent in real terms. Exports in 1976 increased at a 40 per cent rate, due largely to the revival of the American and Japanese economies.

Diversification of exports, it was noted, must turn on the expansion of manufacturers. In this area of performance as well, the Korean experience fits the model of how economic development might often best proceed. A 1969 comparison of the value of manufactured exports as a percentage of total exports made for some twenty-five LDCs revealed that Korea, with 77.1 per cent of its exports consisting of manufactured goods, ranked first, far and away the highest proportion for any country. Some slight relationship was apparent for these countries between per capita GDP and manufactures in export -- richer countries exporting proportionately more manufactured products than poorer countries -- placing the Korean case in even sharper relief, since per capita GDP in Korea was less than the median of the LDCs examined.

For most countries, the proportion of manufactured exports was relatively small: for sixteen countries with per capita GDP of less than $250 in 1969 (the income group in which Korea fell in that year), the proportion was 12.2 per cent; for the nineteen countries with per capita GDP greater than $250, it was 13.5 per cent.[21] In 1970, Korea ranked as the fourth largest producer of manufactured exports among LDCs covered in the survey, with 4.3 per cent of the total, behind only Hong Kong, India and Chile. Total value of its manufactured exports exceeded those of other leading LDC exporters such as Mexico, Singapore, Brazil, Argentina and Indonesia. The fact that Korea accounted for only .27 per cent of world manufactured exports in the same year suggests that its market penetration might well be extended further.[22] In this regard, Gilbert Brown has hypothesized that the demand for an LDCs exports "is elastic for those products in which the country's exports are not a major factor (say 15 per cent) in determining world prices..."[23]

The question of diversification and concentration – the trade structure -- may now be addressed directly. (See Table 3-6.)

In addition to the types of commodities exported and the size and growth of the export sector, a key indicator of development concerns the general structure of trade. It is not unusual among LDCs for one or a few commodities to comprise the great bulk of exports. Such a situation is vulnerable to disruptions in production and to wide fluctuations in demand. High concentrations in exports can be due to many factors. An adequately skilled and disciplined labor force capable of operating the complex technology necessary in modern manufacturing may not exist; international tastes, fashions and qualitative demands may be poorly understood; related infrastructure may not be developed; government policy may be misguided in failing to encourage savings, establish realistic exchange rates, control inflation, or eliminate resource-absorbing subsidies. Avoidance of realistic economic choices is an all too attractive pattern among decision-makers, either because of the short-term personal and political pay-offs attendant on such avoidance, or because of a decision to pursue the ideological will-o'-the-wisp but psychically soothing goal of "social justice" before development has sufficiently proceeded and as if growth was necessarily inimical to welfare in any case.

The 1973 UN study of industrialization and development examined concentration in exports for some thirty-five LDCs.[24] It may first be noted again that Korea had the highest proportion of manufactured products in its total

Table 3-6

Export Concentration in Selected LDCs (1969)

Higher Income Developing Countries ($375 per capita, 1972)	No. commodities exported	No. Manufactured exports	Concentration index	Value of manufactured exports as % of total
Argentina	103	54	.271	7.0
Brazil	120	68	.333	6.2
Chile	49	22	.711	73.0
Cyprus	55	27	.296	9.5
Dominican Republic	33	12	.544	1.6
Guatemala	36	13	.508	1.6
Guyana	28	12	.492	14.7
Jamaica	55	30	.506	19.2
Lebanon	79	46	.392	17.5
Mexico	110	89	.110	19.2
Panama	45	21	.541	10.0
Tunisia	66	28	.210	14.9
Middle Income Developing Countries ($200-375 per capita, 1972)				
Egypt	76	45	.410	11.3
Honduras	25	6	.662	0.9
KOREA	101	71	.276	77.1
Morocco	82	42	.297	6.6
Philippines	75	43	.297	5.0
Thailand	77	38	.243	2.9
Lower Income Developing Countries (under $200 per capita, 1972)				
Afghanistan	17	8	.584	18.7
Central African Rep.	17	4	.351	36.5
Ethiopia	34	13	.534	2.2
Kenya	69	37	.313	10.1
Sri Lanka	37	18	.627	3.5
Tanzania	44	16	.213	2.4
Uganda	26	9	.503	14.7

NOTE: Concentration measured by Hirschman index. Values range from 0 to 1 (maximum concentration). See source below for formula. Commodities grouped as defined in *Commodity Indexes for The Standard International Trade Classification, Revised, Vol. II,* UN publication.

SOURCE : Export data from UNIDO, *Industrial Development Survey,* Vol. 5 (New York, 1973), pp. 53-54; income groupings by *World Bank Atlas,* 1974 classification.

export of all countries surveyed. The *number* of Korean manufactured exports in 1969 numbered 71, a product mix exceeded only by Mexico (89) and approached by Brazil (68). No other LDC even approached these figures. For the 1974 *World Bank Atlas'* middle-income developing countries for which data are available – the group in which Korea fell – comparable figures were: Egypt (45); Honduras (6); Morocco (42); Philippines (43); Thailand (38) and South Vietnam (8). The higher-income developing countries for which data are available, excepting Mexico and Brazil, had the following number of manufactured exports: Argentina (54); Chile (22); Cyprus (27); Dominican Republic (12); Guatemala (13); Guayana (12); Israel (30); Lebanon (46); Panama (21); Tunisia (28). The plight of many of the lower-income developing countries with respect to this aspect of development is apparent from the following comparative figures: Afghanistan (8); Central African Republic (4); Chad (0); Ethiopia (13); Sierra Leone (6); Sri Lanka (18); Sudan (8); Tanzania (16); Uganda (9); Kenya (37). Of this group, only Kenya has achieved reasonable diversity in the number of manufactured products exported.

The Hirschman concentration index for these countries bears a typically close but not invariable relationship to the number of exported manufactured products. The concentration index for Korea in 1969 was a relatively very low .276, for Mexico, which had the lowest index, it was .111. There is also a relationship between concentration ratios and per capita GDP, with Korea being the most obvious exception to this tendency. Korea, which had a per capita GDP of less than $250 in 1969, exported a total of 101 commodities and had a very low concentration ratio for the same year. The impact of the Korean development strategy was profound and altogether exceptional in achieving (1) a large export sector; (2) a large proportion of manufactured products in export; and (3) a low concentration ratio in the export structure, all in a country where, on the basis of per capita GDP alone, predictions concerning these performances would have been very different. Culture and policy, not uncommon opportunities, must be accorded central responsibility for these achievements. Special opportunities have been more widely available in some other areas which, for whatever reasons, have failed to mobilize the resources and make the choices necessary for broad and rapid growth.

Education: Mobilization of Human Resources

It appears that no country in the world with a per capita income level below Korea's exceeds Korea in educational activity and, indeed, that no country which falls approximately near Korea's level of economic development has achieved the level of education of the Korean population.

Around the world, the association of national per capita incomes to educational expenditures was .65 for 28 randomly selected countries in 1965.[25] Table 3-7 shows a coefficient of correlation of .73 between per capita income and education levels among young adults for twenty-six countries for which comparative data were available. These are moderately high correlations, but still leave room for the substantial influence of other factors on educational allocations. Other studies have shown a similar pattern for relationships between GNP and school enrollments (although enrollments in scientific and technical fields, which might be presumed to have particularly important consequences for economic development are only weakly related to GNP).[26] The relationship of education to economic growth has not yet been clarified in the developmental literature, doubtlessly because of difficulty in holding constant the myriad other factors relevant to the process of growth. Moreover, education varies significantly in the design of different societies. In some, education is a means of stabilizing an existing culture; in others it is a means of altering current conditions; in most it is some mix of both.[27] Thus, while the relationship internationally between income and education is reasonably high, it is by no means perfect, and resource constraints do not entirely determine the emphasis that education will receive in a particular country. The nature of its political system is important, as are underlying cultural values.[28]

Whatever the general tendency, Korea is a deviant case from any perspective in its quite remarkable commitment to education. Its school enrollments, for example, are comparable to those often found in countries with per capita income levels twice (and sometimes more) than its own. (See Table 3-7.) In 1970, median years of education in Korea were 6.76 for young adults (ages 25-34) and per capita income was roughly $300, while, for example, in Algeria (per capita income, $430) it was 0.65 years for the same age group; in Zambia ($480) it was 0.97 years, and in Iraq ($370) it was 0.55. Even more striking illustrations emerge from comparisons with several countries which had much higher per capita incomes: e.g., Costa Rica ($630) with 3.92 years median education for the 25-34 age group; Mexico ($750) with a 4.13 years median; Panama ($880) with a 4.81 years median; France ($3,620) with a 5.01 median; and Italy ($1.960) with a 4.05 median, all for the 25-34 age group.

Income elasticity of demand for education in Korea has been very high as well. In 1955, when per capita income was just over $50, median years of education for the 25-34 year age group was 4.52. This may be compared with countries which now have very low per capita incomes but which are typically characterized by far fewer years of education for young adults. In 1961, India, for example, with a per capita income of $110, had achieved a median of only 0.7 years of education for the 25-34 age group.

The same effect is suggested by the relationship between age and education in Korea, one which demonstrates that education has not in fact been traditionally available on a broad scale. The older "colonial" population in Korea – consisting of those 55 years or older in 1970, and hence including those who matured during the period of Japanese rule – had a median educational level of 1.28 years. Those who grew up in the later years of imperial rule and in the early post-World War II period (the 35-34 age group) have a much higher median level of education of 5.74 years. Liberation from Japanese domination, *not* economic growth, unleashed the impulse toward education which had been forced into cultural latency by a half century of foreign occupation. That it was not destroyed tells us something about the resiliency of Korean culture.

Only in vastly wealthier countries – and not always then – do years of education for young adults exceed Korean levels. One cannot assert that the Korean emphasis on education is related unambiguously to economic growth, although some connection undoubtedly exists and will presumably become even more direct as Korea's economy grows in complexity and technical sophistication. It is apparent in any case that the intense commitment to education is seen by large numbers of Korean parents and students as a means to social mobility and a better life. It is an index of the achievement ethic, commented on by many foreign observers, embodied in the Korean culture and which, in the last analysis, is probably a more important factor in development than high levels of material capital investment.[29]

Table 3-7

Per Capita Income (1972) and Median Years of Education of Young Adults (25-34 Age group) for Selected Countries (circa 1970)

	Per Capita Income ($) (a)	Rank (b)	Median Years Education (c)	Rank (d)	Difference Between (b) and (d)
United States	5,590	1	12.54	1	0
Canada	4,440	2	10.06	4	-2
France	3,620	3	5.01	13	-10
West Germany	3,390	4	11.88	2	+2
Israel	2,610	5	8.16	6	-1
Czechoslovakia	2,380	6	10.49	3	+3
Japan	2,320	7	7.84	9	-2
Italy	1,960	8	4.05	16	-8
Libya	1,830	9	0.64	25	-14
USSR	1,530	10	8.12	7	+7
Poland	1,500	11	8.58	5	+6
Argentina	1,290	12	7.39	8	+4
Venezuela	1,240	13	3.16	19	-6
Hong Kong	980	14	6.44	12	+2
Panama	880	15	4.81	14	+1
South Africa	850	16	3.90	18	-2
Chile	800	17	6.70	11	+6
Mexico	750	18	4.13	15	+3
Costa Rica	630	19	3.92	17	+2
Algeria	430	20	0.65	24	-4
Zambia	380	21	0.97	21	0
Iraq	370	22	0.55	26	-4
KOREA	310	23	6.76	10	+13
Kenya	170	24	0.83	22	+2
India	110	25	0.70	23	+2
Indonesia	90	26	2.35	20	+6

NOTE : Coefficient of correlation between (a) and (c), r = .73; R^2 = .53.

SOURCE : Education data from UNESCO *Statistical Yearbook, 1973;* income data from *World Bank Atlas, 1974.*

Table 3-8

Median Years of Education by Age, Sex and Rural/Urban Residence in Korea, 1970

	Age	Median Years	Female
Total Population	25–34	6.76	6.32
	35–54	5.74	5.14
	55+	1.28	0.78
	25+	5.82	5.28
Urban Population	25–34	7.75	6.90
	35–54	6.78	6.04
	55+	3.60	1.16
	25+	6.84	6.16
Rural Population	25–34	6.24	5.92
	35–54	5.12	3.48
	55+	0.94	0.70
	25+	5.16	3.64
Median Years of Education by Age and Sex, 1955			
	15–24	5.65	4.80
	25–34	4.52	3.28
	35–64	2.40	1.12
	65+	0.79	0.63
	25+	2.84	1.72

SOURCE : UNESCO *Statistical Yearbook,* 1973.

Access to education has in recent years been extended throughout Korean society, to rural as well as urban areas and to females as well as males. This is a far cry from the educational disadvantages faced by females and rural people before the developmental thrust of more recent years took place. By 1970, median years of education for the 25-34 age group was 7.75 years in urban areas and 6.24 for rural areas. By the same year, women between 25-34 years old had a median education of 6.32 years, compared to 6.76 years for the entire population of the same age group. Rural women between 25-34 years old had a median education of 5.92 years in 1970, compared to 6.9 years for urban women.

Table 3-9

College Level Fields of Study of Korean Students, 1971

Total Enrollment	Humanities	Education	Fine Arts	Law	Social Science	Natural Science
214,653	19,226 (.09%)	31,423 (14.6%)	8,546 (4.0%)	6,209 (2.9%)	33,639 (15.7%)	15,132 (7.0%)

Engineering	Medical Sciences	Agriculture	Not Specified
55,161 (25.7%)	20,579 (9.6%)	22,201 (10.3%)	2,537 (1.2%)

SOURCE : *UNESCO Statistical Yearbook, 1973.*

The incorporation of rural dwellers and women into the modern educational system over the last twenty years has doubled the years of education for young women (in 1955, median education was only 3.28 years for women between 25-34 years old), and increased schooling for rural dwellers has been similarly dramatic (of rural dwellers over 55 years old, median years of education was 0.94 in 1970).[30] (See Table 3-8.)

It is instructive to observe in this connection that educational activity is presumably (although, as noted, empirical studies are inconclusive) not undifferentiated in its consequences for development and that enrollment ratios alone, while associated with economic devleopment, provide little or no information on the kinds of educational programs that are apt to be most productive in economic terms. There are *prima facie* reasons to suppose, however, that technical training is more important to the industrializing process than education in the fine arts and that medical training is more important than legal education. The imbalance that obtains in some countries between fields of study and their likely contribution to growth does not appear to be a problem in Korea, however. Of the 214,653 students enrolled in college level studies in 1971, only 4 per cent were in the fine arts, 2.9 per cent in law, and 9 per cent in the humanities. These ratios may be compared with the presumably more economically productive enrollments in engineering, for example, which was the course of study of 25.7 per cent of *all* students. Agriculture enrolled 10.3 per cent, medical sciences 9.6 per cent, natural science 7 per cent, education 14.6 per cent, and social sciences 15.7 per cent, all of which are in some ways important to the development process. (See Table 3-9.)

Those benefits from education which extend beyond

simply heightened self-awareness (itself an important objective, of course) can be regarded in economic terms as investment in human resources. Thus, higher expenditure in education is to a considerable degree higher investment in human capital, which in turn implies higher savings. National accounts on savings and investment normally do not include education expenditures, however, and for this reason savings and investment in Korea are in fact considerably higher than a reading of the national accounts alone would suggest.

Population growth

Increases in per capita income are made possible not only by investment levels and the productivity of capital and labor but by reductions in the rate of population growth. Korea, with a population of some 35.9 million in 1976, has one of the highest population densities in the world, some 325 people per square kilometer.[31] Of course, ratios of population to land can be misleading -- a square kilometer can be an industrial or agricultural area, fertile or barren, flat or mountainous, with a favorable or unfavorable climate. Whatever the situation elsewhere, in Korea the problem of population relative to arable land is particularly acute, inasmuch as very little additional land can be brought into cultivation. In spite of the most strenuous efforts, for example, from 1960 to 1970, arable land in cultivation increased only from 2.03 million hectares to 2.3 million hectares and irrigated arable land from 663,000 hectares to 759,000 hectares. Further increments are possible only within narrow limits. Countries that compare with Korea in population per square kilometer include Puerto Rico (264 persons), Egypt (538 persons, excluding desert areas), and Java (400 persons), all of which are far above world (about

30 persons) and regional averages (Africa, 10; North America, 10; Asia, 70, USSR, 9). Population control in Korea, more than in many other developing countries, is imperative if general standards of living are to be increased.

While population pressures will continue to press on the development process, it is significant that here, as in other areas, recent trends are encouraging. For example, annual increases in population averaged 1.9 per cent in Korea during 1965-72. This ratio was 24 per cent less for the same period than that for the developing world as a whole (2.5 per cent average annual increase); 17 per cent less than the average for the higher-income developing countries (2.3 per cent), 30 per cent less than the average for the middle-income developing countries (2.7 per cent); and 24 per cent less than the average for the lower-income developing countries (2.5 per cent). It is 14 per cent less than the average for the world as a whole (2.2 per cent), which includes the very low rates of increase for the industrialized countries (1.0 per cent) and the centrally-planned economies (1.4 per cent, a figure which is inflated by the high growth countries of North Korea and Mongolia with 2.7 per cent increases). (See Table 2-1.)

Korea's performance can be put into further perspective by noting that, of the twenty-one middle-income developing countries ($200-375 per capita income) with population of over one million -- the group in which Korea fell in 1972 -- only Cameroon had as low a rate of population increase. Of the twenty-five lower-income countries, only Chad (1.8 per cent), Gambia (1.9 per cent), Haiti (1.6 per cent), Mauritana (1.9 per cent), and Nepal (1.8 per cent) had similarly low rates of population growth.[32] By 1976, the Korean population growth rate had been reduced to 1.6 per cent and efforts to further reduce the rate were underway. Employment problems will remain for some time, however, as individuals born during the higher growth period enter the labor force.

National Defense

Common sense -- which is often neither common nor sensible -- holds that the defense programs in the LDCs, which in the 1960s grew at a faster average rate than their economies as a whole, retard growth by diverting resources from productive to non-productive activities. The first systematic study of this question, however, came to a much more qualified conclusion and justifies some attention to the contributions that security expenditures may make to growth.[33]

For forty-four LDCs examined by Benoit, the correlations between defense expenditures and growth were in fact positive for the 1950-65 period: high growth countries tended to have high, and low growth countries low, defense burdens.[34] The possibilities that high growth leads to heavier defense burdens, that the data were systematically biased, or that the correlations were spurious were pursued by Benoit and rejected in the first two instances. It was discovered that other factors, principally foreign assistance, did provide part of the answer: foreign aid allowed certain countries (Korea among them) to maintain high levels of defense and, simultaneously, high rates of investment and growth.[35]

Intervening variables were not, however, sufficient to explain all of the variance, and the conclusion seems broadly correct that defense expenditures may very well have positive growth effects which in some circumstances outweigh their negative ones. The net impact of defense expenditures on growth in Korea is in keeping with this observation. Modern defense forces provide training in technical and managerial skills which a growing industrial economy requires; defense programs provide a dual-purpose infrastructure of transportation, communications and other goods and services equivalent to those provided by the civilian economy; defense spending, in the context of inflation and under-employed resources (particularly labor) may increase aggregate demand when government policy seeks to reduce inflation; and, most importantly, national security is a prerequisite for the stability and order essential to induce high and sustained rates of savings and investments. Perceptions of international dangers, which become concretized in large military establishments, may also serve to integrate and mobilize a society around shared purposes and objectives, economic development, itself a source of national strength, among them.

It is of course true that the opportunity costs of defense expenditures might be greater than such benefits as these, but only if optimal rather than actual alternatives are considered. A reduction in defense spending may very well be absorbed by choices which have limited or even negative consequences for growth. This is not to be construed as an argument on behalf of increased defense expenditures. But in the situation in which history has placed South Korea -- a peninsula surrounded by the sea and a hostile, well-armed and aggression-prone regime to the north -- it is important to make a virtue of necessity.

In 1974, Korea spent 4.2 per cent of GNP on defense in order to maintain 620,000 regular troops, a reserve force of 2.5 million, and some 1000 tanks, 400 armored vehicles and 250 combat aircraft. As additional security, 42,000 United States troops were stationed in Korea in early 1978, although the army component is scheduled for withdrawal. The Korean National Assembly has approved a defense tax measure amounting to 25 per cent of total taxes in order to finance a second five-year $5 billion modernization program. The delayed first five-year plan ($1.5 billion, American financed) was to be completed in 1977. The second five-year plan is to be largely financed by Korea itself, although the United States has promised support in the form of loans and other assistance. In Benoit's sample of forty-four LDCs, Korea had the fourth highest proportion of its population under arms and was tenth in its ratio of defense expenditure to GDP; yet its growth rate for 1950-65 was among the highest – and has increased considerably during 1965-75, as already emphasized.[36] Defense spending as a proportion of GNP had, although it is now being increased, not risen since its high of 5.5 per cent in 1953.

Only after the military revolution of 1961 were programs devised for the active involvement of the security forces in economic and social development. This involvement has supplemented more conventional forms of investment, particularly in construction, public health, education and agriculture.[37] Specific activities have included work in navigation, flood damage, tidal land reclamation, food transportation, improvement in rice and barley production methods, fish farm excavations, tree moth eradication and farm harvesting, road construction and repair, epidemic prevention, and medical and dental examinations in villages. Large quantities of equipment and material (trucks, ships, fuel) supplemented the military manpower efforts in such projects. In Benoit's view, however, education of members of the defense forces has probably been the most important contribution of the military to the civilian economy.[38] The very large American contribution to the Korean military program over 1950-65 (165 per cent of the Korean contribution) allowed for the application of defense resources to development, indicating, as Benoit notes, that "Militarily motivated aid has thus been a key element in the Korean success story."[39]

An additional subsidy has been involved as well: although levels of training suggest that military pay should approximate the industrial wage, conscription (for a three year period) has allowed the government to maintain pay and allowances at less than market rates. The scope of conscription is such that the defense forces' subsidization of the supply of merit and public goods is substantial. Thus, official figures for taxation and investment are understated in consequence of the military's contribution to development. The policy decision to orient the Korean deterrent force – which, being a deterrent, accumulates more resources than are actually being used in peacetime -- to developmental purposes has lowered the overhead costs of sustaining them. Together with other developmentally-inclined policies, civic action by the military has made an important if non-obvious contribution to growth over the last decade.

Summary

Capital formation and the efficiency of its use, the mobilization of resources for the provision of public goods and services, export performance, education and population trends are all important to the launching of a stable and expanding economy. Korea has managed a remarkable performance relative to other LDCs on all of these aspects of development. With respect to the increasing level and growth of capital formation in Korea, the role of international demand and foreign loans and investments has been crucial and that of direct government investment increasingly less important. The government's decision costs have been steadily de-centralized to firms and private investors, lowering the risks attendant on public investment decisions and reducing demands on government for uneconomic investment choices.

For the 1950-65 period, savings in Korea were low compared to many other LDCs. Marginal savings ratios, however, were very high, and by 1974 savings as a proportion of GDP were higher (over 25 per cent) than for any other LDC surveyed. Government divestiture policy was implemented on a broad scale and that fact, combined with high rates of private sector investment, reduced the share of government ownership of industrial enterprises. Opportunity cost pricing policies in the remaining public enterprises eliminated inefficient subsidies and pressure on general revenues and allowed for the economic expansion of services (mainly transportation and communications) essential to sustained investment in the goods sector. Monetary policy, international demand, and governmental stability increased material incentives for private savings.

While of limited usefulness, incremental capital output ratios (ICORs) have often been regarded as a measure of the extent to which capital is being efficiently allocated to particular applications. Not only are ICORs normally related inversely to growth, but production patterns vary greatly among countries. Nonetheless, ICORs seem not to be related to levels of development, with poorer countries often having lower ICORs than their presumed needs for infrastructure might suggest. The ICOR for Korea was among the lowest of all LDCs examined, even for those at considerably higher levels of development. The high rate of Korean investment in machinery and equipment -- which is similar to the rate in more developed Latin American countries -- is a partial explanation, as is its export-oriented economic structure.

Mobilization of tax revenues is essential if the supply of

public goods necessary to assist more directly productive activity is to be made available. Cross-national comparisons of tax/GDP ratios as measurements of developmental effort are, however, difficult to make, because activities in different countries are organized variously between the public and private sectors, because the requirements for infrastructure are similarly varied, and because stabilization policy may call for higher or lower revenue collections in given circumstances. Tax revenues in Korea were low among LDCs for the 1950-65 period (thirty-third out of thirty-six comparison countries) at about 9.2 per cent of GDP. Growth in national income produced a high elasticity of growth in tax collections for 1955-65 (1.8, third highest for twenty-two LDCs surveyed) but a very much lower elasticity (.63) for 1960-65 (thirtieth out of thirty-three comparison LDCs). In recent years, tax receipts have stabilized at 17-20 per cent of GNP. Korea can be described accurately as a moderate tax/high growth country. The view that a high rate of public sector mobilization of revenue is essential to growth does not withstand examination: the coefficient of correlation between tax levels and growth for twenty-six LDCs was .095. Whether the social balance maintained in Korea is optimal in terms of growth is not possible to say, although certainly tax policy has not been inconsistent with the high growth rates already observed.

The importance of the export sector for economic growth is widely acknowledged: exports stimulate domestic growth, facilitate specialization and earn foreign exchange to meet import bills. In many LDCs, export earnings derive largely from one or a few primary products and tend to be unstable because of wide fluctuations in international demand and domestic bottlenecks. The expansion of manufactured exports -- in terms both of levels and diversification -- is consequently a key concern of many LDC decision-makers. Among LDCs, Korean rate of growth in total exports was the greatest in the world (excluding the petroleum states) as well as the greatest for manufactured exports during the 1960s and has continued into the 1970s. Foreign debts – which seem to be adequately managed – have nonetheless accumulated quickly because of the soaring international costs of food and petroleum. Diversification of Korean manufactured exports has paralleled the performance in export expansion. The proportion of manufactured products in total exports was the highest (77.1 per cent) of all LDCs in 1969, the number of manufactured exports (71) was exceeded only by Mexico (89). The Hirschman concentration index was also low for Korea, indicating that manufactured exports were not dominated by a few products.

In education, we have noted that no country in the world with per capita income less or comparable to that in Korea exceeds Korea in educational levels, and that the Korean educational pattern approximates that found in countries with per capita incomes twice and sometimes even higher than Korean per capita income. Korean education in fact often approximates European levels. Demand for education in Korea has been remarkably strong and equal access to education has been approximated in recent years between urban and rural areas and between males and females. Third level enrollments have tended to concentrate in technical, managerial, educational, and health specialities and less in fields more remote from developmental applications.

Growth in the economy must outpace growth in population if per capita incomes are to increase, making population trends of key importance in any developmental strategy. Korea, one of the most densely populated countries in the world had, until the 1960s, an extremely high growth rate but managed to reduce population growth to 1.6 per cent in 1976. This more recent growth rate -- while probably still too high -- is less than the average among LDCs, and less than the average for the world as a whole. Among forty-six lower and middle-income developing countries, only six have achieved growth rates comparable to Korea's. Korea's growth rate still exceeds the average among developed countries for the same period (1.0 per cent) but, overall, its population policy has been one of the most successful in the less-developed world.

Contrary to some views, the maintenance of large defense burdens has not been inimical to economic growth, either in Korea or many other LDCs. Korea, it was noted, benefited both from foreign military assistance, a fact which reduced pressure on domestic resources, but has also employed its domestically-supported defense establishment effectively in the production of public goods and services. It seems quite likely that defense expenditures in Korea have had growth effects greater than their negative ones.

The rapid growth in per capita income has thus been accompanied by striking transformations across a broad front of related dimensions. On every index of developmental effort examined, Korea ranks at or near the top in performance among LDCs and often highly developed countries as well. The consistency of these patterns indicate that the Koreans have unlocked the secret -- if that is what it is -- of sustained economic progress by understanding development as involving complementary relationship in many sectors and not merely one of capital formation, or education, or agriculture, or exports, or taxation. The view that development requires the fixing of "priorities" according to some developmental theory which purports to isolate the factors deserving of greatest attention and commitment is, judging from the Korean case, inherently flawed. What seems to be required is a more balanced, system-wide perspective in which the contributions of one sector are seen as inextricably linked to contributions in other sectors. One is not more important nor less important than any other. The policy adjustments which will facilitate growth and linkages in the many spheres bearing on development need not, however, ensue from a grand and comprehensive national plan the construction of which requires immense data and calculations which most ordinary people are not competent to make. The essential problem may be one of establishing systems of incentives by which individuals are encouraged to take self-interested decisions which, in their cumulative effect, construct a social setting conducive to growth.

Notes

1. UNCTAD, *The Measurement of Development Effort* (New York, 1970).

2. *Ibid.*, pp. 17-27.

3. *Ibid.*, pp. 20-21.

4. The Bank of Korea, *Economic Statistics Yearbook* (Seoul, 1975), p. 265.

5. Gilbert T. Brown, *Korean Pricing Policies and Economic Development in the 1960s* (Baltimore: The Johns Hopkins University Press, 1973), pp. 77-78. Still, the Korean public sector is surprisingly large. See Leroy P. Jones, *Public Enterprise and Economic Development: The Korean Case* (Seoul: Korea Development Institute, 1975).

6. *Economic Statistics Yearbook*, 1975, p. 67.

7. *Ibid.*, pp. 78-79.

8. *The Measurement of Development Effort*, pp. 24-25.

9. *Ibid.*, p. 26

10. UNIDO, *Industrial Development Survey*, V. 5 (New York, 1973), p. 80.

11. Harvey Leibenstein, "Incremental Capital-Output Ratios and Growth Rates in The Short Run," *Review of Economics and Statistics*, 48 (February, 1966). The impressive Korean efficiency in the use of domestic and foreign resources is put in cross-national context by Alan M. Strout, "Korea's Use of Foreign and Domestic Resources: A Cross-country Comparison," in Irma Adelman, *Practical Approaches to Development Planning: Korea's Second Five-Year Plan* (Baltimore: The Johns Hopkins University Press, 1969), pp. 277-288.

12. ICORs are from *Industrial Development Survey*, pp. 106-107.

13. *Ibid.*, pp. 108-109.

14. See, for example, L.L. Wade and Robert L. Curry, *A Logic of Public Policy* (Belmont, CA: Wadsworth, 1970).

15. *The Measurement of Development Effort*, p. 29.

16. *Ibid.*, p. 35.

17. *Economic Statistics Yearbook,* 1975.

18. *The Measurement of Development Effort,* pp. 37-38.

19. The Bank of Korea, *Annual Report* (Seoul, 1974), pp. 2-3.

20. Normon Pearlstine, *The Wall Street Journal,* December 1975, p. 32.

21. *Industrial Development Survey,* pp. 53-54.

22. *Ibid.,* p. 16.

23. Brown, *Korean Pricing Policies,* p. 279. These prospects depend to considerable degree not only upon Korean policy and capabilities but also the international trade and investment environment, subjects which cannot be treated in detail here. Traditional trade theory is undergoing revision not only because of the shocks of Leontief's paradoxical results (which confounded comparative cost theory) but also because of new views of the product cycle, technology gaps, uncertainty, and so forth. The now extensive literature on these subjects is surveyed in G. C. Hufbauer, "The Impact of National Characteristics and Technology on the Commodity Composition of Trade in Manufactured Goods," in Raymond Vernon (ed.), *The Technology Factor in International Trade* (New York: National Bureau of Economic Research, 1970), pp. 145-231. Starts toward a reconstruction of traditional theory may be found in G. K. Helleiner, "Manufactured Exports From Less-Developed Countries and International Firms," *The Economic Journal,* vol. 83 (March, 1971), pp. 21-47; and Raymond Vernon, "International Investment and International Trade in the Product Cycle," *The Quarterly Journal of Economics,* vol. LXXX (February, 1966), pp. 191-207. Institutional rules (e.g., item 807.00 of the U.S. tariff regulations, the generalized system of preferences, special in-country concessions) and other factors (e.g., wage rates, skill levels, product cycle trends, communications efficiency, distance, political reliability) suggest that Korea will remain an attractive location for export-oriented foreign investment for some time to come.

24. *Industrial Development Survey,* pp. 52-53. The Hirschmann index, with values from 0 to 1 (maximum concentration) was used.

25. A. J. Groth and L. L. Wade, "International Educational Policy Outcomes," in D. Sijdanskie, *Political Decision-Making Processes* (New York: Elsevier, 1973), p. 130.

26. F. Harbison and C. A. Myers, *Education, Manpower and Economic Growth* (New York: McGraw-Hill, 1964).

27. The perplexing relationship of education and economic growth is considered, e.g., in M. J. Bowman and C. A. Anderson, "Concerning The Role of Education in Development," in C. Geertz (ed.) *Old Societies and New States* (New York: The Free Press, 1963), and A. L. Peasler, "Primary School Enrollments and Economic Growth," *Comparative Education Review* (February, 1967), pp. 57-63. Inconsistencies in the relationship are presumably related to varied performances in other spheres important to growth.

28. Growth and Wade, "International Educational Policy Outcomes."

29. This is the persuasive thesis of P. T. Bauer's *Dissent on Development* (London: Weidenfeld and Nicolson, 1971). By the same token, E. E. Hagen found no relationship between levels of investment and growth for some 75 countries in the early 1960s. See *The Economics of Development* (Homewood, Ill.: Irwin, 1968), p. 183. The UN Study, *The Measurement of Development Effort,* p. 18, examined data for 58 developing countries and revealed that, for the years 1950-65, countries with average annual growth rates of 2.4 per cent or less averaged an investment ratio of 15.7 per cent of GDP, while those with growth rates of 7.5 per cent and over had average investment ratios of 20.2 per cent of GDP. For other countries as well, investment ratios were associated with growth, but rather modestly, and not in all cases.

30. UNESCO, *Statistical Yearbook, 1973.*

31. *The Fourth Five-Year Development Plan* (Seoul: Economic Planning Board, 1976).

32. *World Bank Atlas: Population, Per Capita Product and Growth Rates* (Washington, D. C., 1974).

33. Emile Benoit, *Defense and Economic Growth in Developing Countries* (Boston: Lexington Books, 1973).

34. *Ibid.,* p. 2.

35. *Ibid.,* p. 3.

36. *Ibid.,* p. 239.

37. *Ibid.,* p. 249.

38. *Ibid.,* p. 248.

39. *Ibid.,* p. 250.

Chapter 4

National Planning: Obstacles, Strategies and Achievements

In any society the public policy process consists in a host of independent and interdependent decisions taken by individuals who maintain shared, overlapping or contradictory preferences both with respect to the nature of the process itself and with respect to the outcomes which if produces.

The decisions involved in the policy process are of three kinds: (1) choices by individuals of their own ends; (2) choices by individuals of the means by which their ends can be achieved; (3) choices by individuals of rules of behavior which constrain others as well as themselves. The first type of choice is a matter of psychology and personal philosophy and can be evaluated only in terms of an ethical value system which, often, will not command universal agreement. The second type of choice (that of selecting means for the achievement of individual ends) involves a technical problem in economizing. Given any particular end, one (or more) means will be relatively more efficient in attaining the end than other means.

The third type of choice is of a political character and involves what may be called questions of *public choice.* Public choices concern the interests of all: they are choices which are pre-emptory and binding throughout a society. Typically, such choices take the form of authoritative *rules* which specify the framework within which individuals may or must conduct their activities. The precise effect of these rules at the level of individual citizens cannot usually be predicted and, normally, the rules are aimed at achieving certain generalized social results. An increase or reduction in interest rates has an impact on consumption/investment patterns by inducing individuals, in their own interests, to adjust their expenditure decisions one way or another. Whether the rule has "worked" or not will be determined by the aggregate economic data collected for just such purposes. The process by which such rules are set is nearly identical with the public policy process itself. It will be observed that the three types of choice identified above are intertwined in the public policy process. Aims of political decision-makers include both personal and social dimensions and it is difficult analytically to determine which set of ends -- personal or public -- are being advanced by the means chosen.

This problem aside, however, one may note that the policy sciences, to the extent that they focus on problems of efficiency in social goal attainment, are non-controversial science. Few if any people are prepared to argue on behalf of wasting scarce resources, which is precisely what inefficiency entails. Problems of social objectives, however, are shot through with conflict and dissensus. These are the subjects of political science and classical economics. In Korea, aspirations for survival, independence, unification, democracy and economic development have been widely if not universally shared for decades and, since the end of World War II and the division of Korea into two antagonistic polities, national policy in the Republic of Korea has been directed to these several objectives in a more or less sequential fashion. Thus, survival of the cultural integrity of the Korean people in the face of the historic Chinese,

Japanese and Russian tendencies or efforts at absorption concerned virtually all politically articulate Koreans in the nineteenth and twentieth centuries and even before. The twentieth century drive for independence from Japan was a means to secure the ancient goal of cultural survival and political independence. Independence from the less direct but no less real influence stemming from the unique convergence of the great power interests of China, the Soviet Union, Japan and the United States in the Korean peninsula is a continuing problem in the struggle for national integrity.

The political division of Korea, which grew out of the zones of occupation established by the U.S.S.R. and the U.S. at the end of World War II, similarly united all Koreans against the permanent separation of a nationality that had been formed by the political integration of the peninsula under the Silla Kingdom in the seventh century. The costs in human life that were born by nationals of several nations in the tragic and misguided effort to unite Korea by force during 1950-53 indicate the extent to which some were prepared to go to achieve unification. A quarter of a century later, the chances of peaceful unification remain as remote as ever, and the possibility of another attempt by the north to unify the country by force an ever-present reality. Within the context of a divided motherland and an unstable international order, the goals of unification and full independence are remote prospects. They remain vital elements in the ideology and strategic behavior of all Korean partisans, however, and, as such, figure importantly in the policy process in South Korea (and North Korea, as well). The emphasis that men of affairs in Korea are willing to accord these objectives varies substantially, particularly when ranked along with other major objectives, namely, the building of a democratic polity and a productive economy. Moreover, varied emphasis is given by activist opinion to the terms and conditions under which these major goals might be achieved. Unification under domination of the totalitarian communism of the north has no measurable support in the south and full independence from great power politics is not something to be managed by any small country, much less one in Korea's situation.

Within the limit of national security requirements, social consensus exists in Korea on the goals of erecting a prosperous and democratic society. But ranking of these objectives varies significantly among South Koreans: democracy and rapid economic growth are viewed by some as improperly ranked by the South Korean government, which has identified economic development (national security excepted) as its highest social priority. Some segments of South Korean intellectual opinion have made opposite choices, asserting either that free democracy (involving more popular participation in governance and the extension of civil liberties) is either properly prior to or not inconsistent with rapid economic development.

Thus, the same bundle of social objectives may be understood differently and ranked variously by partisans in the policy process. Disagreement on the nature and ranking of these items on the public policy agenda are not susceptible to resolutions through technical means. Technical or economic reasoning may produce alterations in individual preferences, however, if it can be shown that the probabilities assigned by an individual to the achievement of his various preferences are in error. Thus, by way of illustration, at least some advocates of a broadened democracy in Korea concluded, following the short-lived experiment under the 1960-61 Chang Myon government, that liberal democracy in Korea is, at least for the time being, not feasible.[1] This view receives persistent challenge on the other hand from those who insist that the Chang experiment did not produce only or even the chaos of a benign but undisciplined democracy but, in fact, had some economic achievements and substantial prospects.[2]

Thus, what is conceptually an empirical question entirely, (e.g., was or was not the Chang government's democratic conduct consistent with national security and orderly and rapid socio-economic development) becomes in fact a question which takes on an ideological coloration. That the question is answered in the affirmative by some and in the negative by others is only evidence that the answer to the question will be conditioned by one's political values. Disagreements among scholars and partisans over the "actual" imperatives and achievements of any government are as apt to turn on personal preferences and biased data as full empirical knowledge of actual conditions. In any case, the overriding objective of the South Korean government has been economic development since the military revolution of May, 1961, security objectives excepted.

It was this goal that gave rise to the (ultimately compromised) economic and social development five-year plan promulgated in January, 1962, a scheme under which GNP was to be increased by over 40 percent during the planning period. The consequences of the decisions embodied in that and the Second Five-Year Plan (1967-71), as well as those of the *ad hoc* economic decisions accompanying them, have by now been impressively studied and described.[3] This, and the Third (1972-76) Five-Year Plan are discussed later in this chapter. Before turning to these matters, however, attention is directed to other aspects of the logic of choice.

Public Choices

In large measure, governments can be viewed as extremely complex groupings of decision rules, or rules which describe what is to be done by whom under particular circumstances. The viability and efficiency of these rules can only be evaluated in terms of the ends which they serve. Political authorities in all societies determine the ends and establish the rules by which the behavior of others as well as themselves will be directed to activities consistent with those ends. For one to assert that the political authorities bear responsibility for the achievement of declared objectives is to say that they have control over the rules which influence or direct human behavior. To change the governmental structure is to invoke new or different rules which, in the view of the decision-makers, are expected to have performance characteristics somehow superior to the old rules.

In making rules on behalf of their strategic objectives, it is necessary that those objectives themselves be expressed operationally as sets of rules: that is what a plan is. Consequently, the policy problem for rational policy-makers consists in trying to choose an optimal set of rules for the achievement of their policy objective. It is with respect to this type of problem that the methods and paraphernalia of applied social science have limited relevence.

If all alternative rules and the costs of applying them were known, the task of selecting the "proper" rules for the achievement of specified aims would be resolved. The most efficient rules not involving unacceptable moral transgressions would be selected. This outcome could be witnessed, however, only when all uncertainty has been eliminated; it could be approached when uncertainty is limited; but it would be rare when uncertainty is pervasive. The latter situation in varying degrees is normal to governments. As a practical matter, governments rarely enjoy the luxury of choosing the "most" efficient way of conducting any activity.

Moreover, no partial solution to the problem of efficient public choices is possible in the absence of a general solution. Governments have multiple objectives; an efficient set of rules governing one sector of aims cannot be established unless efficient rules are known for all sectors. Uncertainty and the interdependence of efficiency requirements confront governments with intractable problems of choice. In real circumstances, the aids to governmental calculations developed in the applied social sciences have limited (but by no means unimportant) uses. Rational individuals who seek to maximize total net benefits (whether understood as utility, welfare, satisfaction, or profits) must follow the rule of applying their resources to activities which have the greatest net marginal rates of return. But exchanges of resources for benefits at the individual as well as collective level are not, among other things, always consumated immediately. Not only must exchanges be entered into which yield benefits to be enjoyed in the present, but some thought must be given to investments which will intendedly yield benefits in the future. Expected future benefits are always subject to discounting, with larger discounts being assigned to longer time periods. By taking appropriate discounts on future benefits, an individual or government can compare present and future benefits and allocate available resources reasonably efficiently.

As we have noted, however, uncertainty often intervenes. Information about present and future returns may be sparse and unreliable. Moreover, in comparing alternatives, a common denominator is required. Without such a denominator, net benefits from various allocations could not be computed and it would be nonsense to speak of net benefits at all. The existence of such a denominator, however, is more a presumption than a fact -- although it is an indispensable fiction which *rational* governments as well as individuals must maintain. The notion of a homogeneous denominator is required by any decision based on a recognition of limited resources and "net" welfare, and is thus central to any idea of rational choice, public or private, individual or institutional. Finally, precisely correct discounts against the future cannot in most cases be discovered by any existing formula. In some markets, economic discounts are known, of course, but even these rest on certain aggregate and gross judgments about what the future holds in store. In all circumstances, prophecies must be made concerning the stability of social, political and economic relationships which are often based as much on hope as on knowledge. Again, this is as much a problem for governments as for individuals. Indeed, the problem is compounded for governments -- because citizens will often prefer present to future enjoyment -- when they must develop rules that encourage individual self-denial. Actually, even governments are biased (rationally so) against the future. Politicians and planners, like everyone else, live in the present and are concerned with their current power, status and income. Long-run pay-offs from governmental decisions may thus have limited relevance not only to citizens generally but to decision-makers as well.[4] Still, the point must be emphasized: while free markets cannot reach a Pareto optimum state when public goods and non-market interdependencies are involved, governmental intervention will not guarantee the achievement either. In a free enterprise economic system, capital flows tend to establish the same discount rate for all markets as investors move their capital until the marginal profit rate is the same in all sectors, including those involving future returns. At this point, a conceptual possibility only, economic equilibrium or a Pareto optimum, has been attained. This outcome is not even conceptually possible for governmental planners, however, a fact which gives sharp contrast to the nature of individual and public choices, and is due in part to the characteristics of so-called public goods.

Public goods will not usually be produced and distributed by market institutions because, once made available, they can be consumed by all, even by those who paid nothing toward their provision. If the benefits which such goods provide are to be forthcoming, only the government (which can coerce contributions from beneficiaries of the goods) can generate them. An important consequence of this is that, for the most part, no Pareto optimum state can be achieved voluntarily when public goods are involved. The welfare of citizens can be enhanced, and a Pareto optimum reached, at least in principle, only if the government acts coercively to provide collective benefits which are otherwise unobtainable.[5]

Moreover, the market cannot take advantage of economies which could be secured through the removal of so-called non-market interdependencies. Only the government is in a position to, let us say, bribe an offensive industry to eliminate its noxious odors, thereby improving property values and the quality of life in the vicinity. Governmental intervention is necessary because no single citizen or voluntary group could or would pay the bribe necessary to change the industry's practices. Unless government intervenes, we again note, no Pareto optimum state can be achieved. Indeed, there are conditions under which it will be in the immediate political interest of a government not to reach such a state and to perform therefore in a socially sub-optimal fashion. Further, there will be arguments that, under certain conditions, sub-optimal choices of this sort may be superior ethically to choices which do achieve Pareto optimality.

As a matter of fact, something less than Pareto optimal solutions may be preferred by individuals if they regard a Pareto solution as potentially damaging in the long run. In addition, demands for equity and redistributions may, to be satisfied, require that government adopt clearly non-Pareto optimum policies. Efficiency is only one goal among many and its full or approximate realization may conflict with other goals, such as democratic participation, national independence or an understanding of social justice which, however attractive, is apt to be less universally accepted than the weak ethical standards of the Pareto test. Regardless of one's preferences in these matters, however, there is no gainsaying the fact that *any* policy choice that sacrifices economic efficiency to some other, and presumably more important objective, will impose net sacrifices on some portion of the community -- this fact should be kept in mind by well-intentioned people who view choices between equity and efficiency as involving the "public interest" in the first instance and "special privilege" in the second. By the same token, choices for efficiency need not necessarily or even probably be destructive of equity goals.

At the individual level, choices between and among several alternatives (consumption, leisure, hoarding, investment) can be made so as to maximize expected satisfaction, and individual rationality can prevail so long as the matters of public goods and non-market interdependencies do not intrude. In all societies, however, the supply of public goods is never precisely calibrated to what quantity of such goods would be demanded by each citizen given the costs to the individual of supplying them. No institution exists by which governments can impose costs and supply public goods at levels consistent with individual preferences. For such reasons, it is difficult to know what is meant by rational decision-making at the collective level once the public goods question has arisen,[6] and when we realize that any government will find it difficult/impossible to make choices which unequivocally improve social welfare. For governments to act on the Pareto principle, accurate "signals" from the citizenry are necessary. Such cues are, as a practical matter, unattainable, even through highly refined mechanisms of popular mobilization and articulation.[7] There is another reason (an additional consequence of uncertainty) why governments may not move society to a Pareto optimal position, namely, because the rules necessary to do so will neither be accepted or invoked for fear that, on some subsequent occasion, the same rules may be employed not on behalf of an unequivocal good but in order to exploit some portion of society.[8] The rules which may improve everyone's position, or someone's without damaging anyone else's may be foregone, then, because of the fear that what is gained at one point may involve greater loses at another.

The Functions of Governmental Choices

It is now possible to point up several implications of

the foregoing discussion. The most important observation to be made is that no Pareto optimal state can be attained by governments for both conceptual and practical reasons. Governments are not, then, engaged in the making of unequivocally good (Pareto optimal) decisions no matter how open, refined and responsive to public impulses they may or wish to be. This conclusion applies to the economically developed liberal democracies of the West as well as to every other type of political system, including that of Korea. This point must be insisted upon and its significance for the evaluation of governmental decisions and public planning underscored. Governments cannot be evaluated in terms of a social welfare function derived from the rational choices of individuals concerning their own welfare. Whatever governments do will, with rare exceptions, damage the interests of some, not only on those occasions when resources are redistributed deliberately, but in cases involving public goods and non-market interdependencies as well.

There are, then, few if any purely economizing choices available to governments interested simply in responding to the citizenry by providing collective goods and opportunities in the degree to which individuals are prepared to support them. Governments must themselves establish social priorities and make allocations for them, choices which cannot fully meet the tests of rationality understood as choices which equalize marginal social returns from all distributions from scarce resources. By the same token, individuals are thrown into a state of decisional disequilibrium as a consequence of their dealings with government, since they cannot know the precise returns, if any, from such interactions.

Efforts to establish an authentic connection between

individual and social objectives, by discovering appropriate political rules for linking them, have proliferated in recent years.[9] These efforts in political economy or public choice are, in one way or another, concerned with the fundamental problem in welfare economics of determining unambiguously whether society is "better off" in one state rather than another. The device usually analyzed in this effort as concerns governmental behavior is the franchise which, under varying conditions, is by presumption allocated to competing politicians in exchange for various public policies. Unfortunately, the search for the rules which would produce a "social welfare function" has reached a compromised conclusion.[10] To assign influence on the basis of "one person, one vote" is to assign (equal) weights to the value accorded to each person's preferences. While not unattractive normatively, it does involve the psychologically unsound practice of interpersonal welfare comparisons. Moreover, and perhaps more importantly, there is no decision rule, democratic or otherwise, which will always/usually aggregate the preferences of individuals into a transitive social welfare function when those preferences are diverse and when the choice is more than two-fold.[11]

It is, consequently, fallacious to believe that there can be discovered either an optimal or socially neutral set of rules by which public policy might be made. That reformers persist in the effort to find and establish such rules is not evidence that such rules exist in principle. For these several reasons, the quality of public policy cannot be evaluated in terms of any universally compelling standard of rationality. A government's development plan, similarly, must be judged on other grounds. But it is by no means intellectually pleasing to forego a scheme which recognizes that resources are scarce, that in a world of considerable pain and suffering.

wasting those resources is intolerable, and that waste can be eliminated only when benefits from all applications of those resources are balanced on all margins. On the other hand, we are not Gods. Political economy cannot tell us that society is better or worse off now or then, or whether government should or should not undertake any particular act. Hortative counsel for governments will have to come from other sources and it may be guaranteed that such advice will not be persuasive to all people. Policy advise from international "experts," who do not have to live with the consequences of their recommendations, is particularly suspect in these matters.

Non-formal obstacles to rational resource allocation can also be identified. Among the most important of these are the institutions of choice and implementation themselves. Authority, power, and information are often distributed among institutions in such a way that program comparisons are made only with difficulty or not at all. Rigidities in administration may make impossible the simultaneous analysis of the costs and benefits of all programs. Some programs are relatively "uncontrollable" – those mandated by law, for example, or those which involve the viability of the government itself, such as servicing the public debt. Fixed charges, partially completed projects, implied commitments of one sort of another, all reduce the latitude within which governments can exercise discretion in the allocation of resources. Reducing the institutional restraints on choice is a continuing problem for governments.

In addition, there are profoundly important methodological and computational obstacles to optimal public choice. Establishing the "proper" discount rate for public projects is, as we have observed, essential to rational analysis. The criterion for setting the public discount rate – the rate of returns available in the private sector – is easy enough to promulgate. Actually, because of imperfections and risks in the marketplace, the opportunity costs of withdrawing resources from the private to the public sector will vary with the private sector from which they are withdrawn. Since capital is never allocated optimally in the private sector, it cannot be allocated optimally in the public sector. A possible way out of this problem is to establish a public discount rate on the basis of the weighted average of the returns on investment in the several productive private sectors. Even so, problems would remain, not the least of which is the difficulty of discovering, because of the complexity of financial activities, the rates of returns in various sectors which obtain in the first place. There are many facets to the public management of risk and uncertainty. If market imperfections make governments *uncertain* about an appropriate discount rate, *risks* in different sectors of the economy may explain (partially) the variable rates of return in those sectors. Thus, whether imperfection and/or harmony explain the situation in the real world becomes itself a source of governmental uncertainty and an obstacle to rational resource dispensations.

A second and related methodological problem consists, as noted, in assigning values to public goods and services allocated by non-market or monopolistic institutions. Efforts to construct public sector analogues to the market have entailed the use of shadow pricing for public goods and services, with necessarily limited success but sometimes good effect (as in Korea). Shadow prices – based on simulations of what willing buyers would pay – require first that large and competitive markets exist for comparative purpose. This condition does not exist anywhere perfectly and less so in smaller countries with, for many goods, emergent markets only. The "efficiency" of simulated markets in the public sector is difficult to gauge; estimates must suffice. Moreover, governments do and must consider nonpecuniary questions in assigning values: the quantity and quality of health care, education and social security involve not only pecuniary judgments as to how expenditures in each of these areas relate to economic development. Pricing of these goods must also entail, as well known, any redistributive goals of government and, as less well known, the impact of their supply on the political system, including its capacity to maintain public order, social continuity and personal freedom. Shadow prices will always be, in greater or lesser degree, "incorrect". They may nonetheless be very useful as a practical matter in policy planning.

The purpose of the foregoing discussion is not to denigrate efforts at systematic policy analysis, much less to belittle the intentions of those concerned to advance social welfare in Korea or other societies. Rigor must be insisted upon in these matters, however, if the opportunities as well as the limits faced by governments are to be assessed correctly. The unavoidable fact is that the individualism underlying the economist's concept of social welfare is a conceptually uncertain and operationally imperfect guide to public policy and resource mobilization and allocation problems. One should recognize that alternative guides – e.g., the political scientist's concept of the "public interest" – is no less flawed. That concept does, however, introduce another dimension to policy analysis which might be raised briefly.

Social Welfare and The Public Interest

For the orthodox economist, optimal social welfare consists in the successful aggregation of individual valuations. As we have just noted, there are many obstacles to that aggregation, obstacles so varied and profound that no actual state of affairs can meet the requirements of the concept. For some political scientists, the concept of the "public interest" functions as a roughly equivalent test of public policy. The operational definition of the public interest, however, is much less precise than that assigned by economists to the notion of social welfare, and varies with the philosophical school to which the political scientist subscribes.[12] Whatever else one may mean by the public interest, it must include, as Flathman notes, a consideration of "... the full impact of the [policy] measure" and the normative considerations relevant to justifying that impact."[13]

That the full impact *cannot* in principle be apprehended, even if practical problems could be overcome, is, as discussed above, a major conclusion of welfare economics, and both similar and additional problems are involved in applying public interest tests in policy-making and evaluation. As used in most political discourse, the public interest is a term used to justify, rationalize, commend or condemn, depending upon whether the speaker approves or disapproves of a particular actual or proposed public policy. In no case, however, does the concept solve the general problem that governments face in evaluating systematically various possible allocations of costs and benefits to the community. The "public interest" is even less useful to governments than the "social welfare function" because the criteria that must be satisfied for an allocation to have been in the public interest are never specified in a manner helpful to them. The criteria as often used are so broad as to lack practical significance or so particularized and partial as to have no general applicability.[14]

So-called "rationalist" public interest theory, which seeks to establish rules of action by which governments can translate preexisting individual preferences into public policy confronts the same criticisms raised against welfare economics and normative political economy. Political scientists writing in this tradition have sought, among other things, to strengthen (weaken) political parties, weaken (broaden) interest group activity, change (preserve) the rules by which political authority is captured and legitimate and binding decisions are made. The search is always for "value-neutral technical processes" by which the "Public Will" can become known and implemented.[15]

Whether these efforts take the form of naive commitments to simple majoritarianism or to more sophisticated and complex institutions and rules, the result, unavoidably, is to stumble into the obstacles to aggregation discussed earlier.[16] This problem of the public interest is insoluable so long as it rests on individualistic assumptions. The quest for criteria which transcend the summation of individual interests and identify values such as "justice", "freedom", "order", "dignity" as the proper objectives of public policy is an ancient one in philosophy and, perhaps, finds its most influential expression in the idealist tradition associated with Plato. The Platonic test of the public interest (which is much like the Confucian test) -- to do justice -- requires that the decision-maker possess an insight into the "essential" nature of justice. This presupposes philosophical understandings which cannot be widely shared -- wisdom not being universally distributed -- and which cannot be given unequivocal operational meaning. More utilitarian concepts of justice may not be "wrong", any more than the economist's social welfare concept is wrong, but are even less helpful when the practical problem of government is to allocate scarce resources among many intrinsically meritorious ends.[17]

The obstacles to rational policy-making discussed above are universal among decision-makers in all societies. In developing countries, where market mechanisms are not always available to perform allocative functions and where resource constraints are profound, the burden of decision-making is particularly heavy. The task is made more difficult still by the typically formative character of the post-colonial political culture and political institutions, which, in the Korean case, have had opportunity to develop only in recent years, and even then under intense external pressure.

Basic Choices in Economic Development

The profound problems of theory and calculation that all governments face in efforts to improve social welfare must, then, be emphasized. No government, it was observed, can possibly base its decisions on the efficiency criterion along (equity calculations are as difficult) and, in the political realm, in consequence, citizen sovereignty must give way to the sovereignty of the political decision-maker. Not only is it *impossible* for the decision-maker to respect all individual calculations of welfare, it is probably inappropriate for him to seek to do so at all, if only because the population whose views are to be conceptually respected in the economist's welfare formulation or the political scientist's public interest scheme are not (cannot be) precisely identified for reasons already given, but also because that population must include not only present but future members of society as well. Because of this, it is the view of some that the more appropriate function of a government is not to respect each individual's preferences but to use its coercive power to achieve collective or social policies which individuals recognize as within the proper sphere of governmental action and authority.[18]

From this perspective, it is not individual utility that government need aggregate but something more vague but no less meaningful – acceptance, tolerance, hope, trust, influence, forbearance. A grant of authority by a people to government may be withdrawn, as it was when the Rhee government lost its "Mandate of Heaven" in 1960, but considerable discretion normally rests with government to identify social goals and the means for their achievement. Such a view provides no test of "proper" governmental action in any unambiguous sense, nor does it vest any particular policy with special status, nor does it mean that whatever government does is appropriate as long as its authority is not eroded in the process. It does mean that nothing succeeds like success. In Korea, as in other, and especially developing, societies, governmental action to provide order and to stimulate economic growth is required of any legitimate authority.

Any nation which aspires to rapid economic development must accomplish two rather dissimilar things at once. In the first place, it must erect institutional mechanisms through which decisions relating to various economic matters can be compared and coordinated for consistency of effect and by which centralized solutions on appropriate mobilization and allocational issues can be found and implemented. In the second place, however, it must stimulate the energies of individuals in all economic and many social sectors to purposeful and desired activities, in short, to decentralize decision-making but within a set of rules provided by central authority. The "best" line between centralized and decentralized decision-making cannot be drawn precisely on the basis of abstract principles but must be adjusted continually in terms of specific problems. The market can be an important aid in this task, as it has been in Korea, but, particularly in smaller and less developed economies, the market is often an imperfect social decision-maker. Indeed, the *creation* of markets must itself be an important objective of the central authority in mixed economies. The effective performance of government as coordinator of basic decisions is indispenable to development. There are a number of key questions which the government must address through its central authority.

Among them, for example is (1) the management of foreign exchange. If scarce foreign exchange is allocated improvidentially to current consumption, needed capital goods cannot be imported. By the same token, regulation of economic activity which has the effect of reducing exports has the same consequences. (2) There are many forms of social overhead which must be supplied if growth is not to be limited -- schools, ports, roads, public utilities -- which either will be supplied not at all by private enterprise or, if supplied, provided in insufficient degree, either because sufficient capital is unavailable to private organizations to carry out the prospective activity, because revenues will not cover costs, because returns are too far in the future, or because the risk of inefficient governmental regulation is perceived as too great. A public authority must, therefore, either finance, organize and supply goods such as these directly or it must do so in part and, at the same time, develop the rules and incentives which will allow private organizations to provide the rest. (3) Fiscal and monetary policy also obviously require central calculation in the light of growth objectives. The consequences of taxation and expenditure decisions for public sector capital formation and private investment/consumption decisions must be assessed. Excessive public and private demand on a nation's scarce resources stimulates the inflation that is chronic to many developing (and developed) societies, erodes incentives and confidence and reduces savings and investment. On the other hand, inadequate rates of taxation inhibit the capacity of the central authority to play its essential role in increasing the nation's capital stock and in achieving its welfare objectives. In a practical planning context, there are no precise criteria for organizing decisions on these matters.

By way of illustration, and without digressing into a technical discussion, capital formation, as defined in national income accounting procedures, refers to additions to a nation's material goods obtained by the expenditure of current product. How one should distinguish between capital goods -- goods used in production -- and other goods follows no completely satisfactory rule. It is conventional in accounting, however, to *omit* from capital goods all consumer (except dwellings) and military (e.g., billets, bases) durables because neither households nor the military are regarded as producers of economic goods and services. Expenditures on social services are also omitted, even though investments in health, education, and security often have important consequences for productivity. Expenditures on the institutions of public choice -- rationalizing the bureaucracy, improving institutional coordination, improving decisional and managerial techniques -- which are essential to economic growth, are also, by convention, not regarded as capital investments. These exclusions facilitate national accounting but do not resolve many practical problems which confront decision-makers, who, for example, must recognize that expansion in the stock of knowledge or improvement in public health is related to productivity but cannot be certain as to the precise consequences for growth of varying levels of expenditure on education, health, etc.[19] Moreover, the historical relationship of capital formation to economic growth in different societies reveals such a tangled statistical picture as to be of limited utility to national decision-makers as a guide to policy. Historic rates of savings and investments in the developed nations are not, as a rule, particularly impressive, which means that history provides few policy guidelines to contemporary systems seeking rapid development. Some capital goods are superior bearers of technological advance than are others, but the "better" patterns for achieving such advances are rarely if ever known or, if known, necessarily capable of being implemented. The ratios of capital formation to aggregate product, which have received so much international attention as a planning tool, have historically varied greatly across societies and show that relatively low rates of investment may be associated with high rates of growth in productivity (as in Japan in the nineteenth century) and that, alternatively, high rates of saving may be associated with relatively low rates of growth (as in Germany for the same period).[20]

It is normally appropriate policy, of course, for public decision-makers to seek those investments which will produce the lowest possible capital-output ratios, but the manner in which this is best accomplished is not an entirely technical matter. Resting to some extent on uncertainty and hence intuition, policy choices must involve risks, given the recognition that the aggregate capital-output ratio for the society will be made up of ratios of various economic sectors which may deviate significantly from the mean.

Intersectoral comparisons are required, the appropriate rule being to shift investment flows from high to low capital-output sectors. Such shifts should not, however, be based on cross-sectional comparisons only: capital-output ratios need not be stable over time -- may either rise or fall – depending, among other things, on the natural history of the sector under review.

Other problems relate to the monetary system, including exchange rates, interest rates, money supply and pricing policies, which must operate effectively if voluntary savings are to be attracted, inflation controlled, exports expanded and general stability established. Education must be provided in sufficient degree. High rates of capital formation and heightened capital and labor productivity will not by themselves increase per capita product if population growth outstrips absolute increases in output. Consequently, a population policy is required in most developing countries if economic objectives are to be realized.

The problems associated with coordinating and implementing policy decisions across such a broad front of intermingled issues are staggering. Data gaps, computational and administrative difficulties, the lack of a social or economic theory that would provide unambiguous decision-rules in concrete cases are inherent in the situation, as are the formidable political problems of gaining acceptance and legitimacy, providing order, and generating and focusing social energy. Successful policy, when developed, is always tentative and may be inadequate for the future. Pressure on the policy system is intense and unrelieved and may prove beyond the control of even extremely able and flexible administrators and politicians. In the best of circumstances, then, the obstacles to sustained economic development are many and profound. That it has occurred at all in history is the remarkable thing; that it has been launched in Korea, where initial prospects seemed particularly bleak, is of special interest in view of the aspirations of people in other unpromising environments.

Inspection of that achievement -- characterized by world leading performances in virtually all sectors thought important to economic development -- might lead to the expectation that growth has stemmed from the effective implementation of a comprehensive and integrated plan in which goals have been clarified and stated, trends and conditions accurately understood and described, and alternative policies for improving performance discovered, evaluated, selected and applied in a systematic fashion. At the same time, failed or compromised policies would, expectedly, have been appraised and modified or terminated as required by the planners' objectives. The evidence is that success in national policy planning does explain much of the Korean case, and that rational analysis has loomed very much larger in Korean decision-making than in many other countries. The Korean genius seems to have consisted in erecting a generalized framework of rules within which the specific and self-interested decisions of individuals to work, save, invest, study, plan and so forth--qualities always available in East Asian society--have been aggregated into a social outcome which fits the requirements of development.

Comparative National Planning

Few subjects among developmentalists generate more interest or controversy than the subject of national planning. In the so-called socialist or non-market economies governed by Marxist-Leninist political parties, development has been sought through detailed central planning by which resources are generated, mobilized, allocated, and coordinated by administrative command and hierarchy. Growth has of course occurred under this system, although it has become increasingly obvious that detailed central planning, as in the Soviet Union, has given rise to very serious micro-economic irrationalities and inefficiencies.[21] In China, the carbon-copy adoption of the Russian model in the early 1950s led to the first (and only detailed published) five-year plan (1953-57) which stipulated overall goals (heavy industry, new industrial areas in the interior); translated them into targets (value and physical units) for each sector and major industy; governed prices (through annual quarterly and monthly plans). Targets involved output, costs, raw material inputs, labor (number, wages and productivity), and profits. Technically, over 700 commodities were to be coordinated by a scheme ("material balances planning") which resembles sectoral planning and input-output analysis. Controls were exercised through various plant-level incentives, budgeting and banking authorities, and focused administrative authority.[22] The centralization of decision-making in Peking apparently proved inconsistent with objective conditions and the altered goals of the political leadership. In 1957-58, emphasis was placed on decentralization, small, labor-intensive industrial plants, decontrols on the allocation of some lesser materials, plant-level committee management, and devolution of central control to provincial and local governmental units. Nonetheless, planning is still carried out in physical terms and the formal system itself (even after the Cultural Revolution) apparently remains intact.[23] At the end of 1976, the PRC had gone through four five-year plans none of which, according to Perkins, has "... played a very important role in directing the Chinese economy."[24] Although hard data are lacking, performance seems rarely to have reflected plans and planning was itself disrupted by the Great Leap Forward and the Cultural Revolution. Long-term detailed planning was, in practice, rejected in favor of annual and shorter term directives.[25] The costs of short-term *ad hoc* planning may have been less than the major "mistakes" unavoidably imbedded in comprehensive, centralized, detailed, largely physical planning arising from the complexity of the calculations to be made, poor and limited data and misjudgments on sector balances. The principal virtue of long-term planning is that, if properly done, it can provide growth targets and an investment scheme for realizing those targets efficiently. In the absence of a market mechanism, continuing signals on investment efficiency are not available, and the problem of shifting resources in more socially optimal directions during the period of the plan as changing circumstances suggest is difficult at best.

In the Soviet Union, inefficiencies in planning have led to the demand for ever more sophisticated techniques (e.g., integrated linear programming) as a solution to the optimization problem, reforms which would have the intended effect of introducing well-known precepts of Western efficiency economics into the planning process.[26] These techniques usually presuppose decentralization of decision-making to the enterprise level, material incentives and the use of shadow pricing as an analogue to the interaction of demand and supply in the market place. The argument for this approach (sometimes called "perfect indirect decentralization") in the Soviet Union, a developed country, and, in developing China, the resort to short-term and decentralized choice-making, point up the profound difficulties involved in genuinely comprehensive planning in two very different countries where it has been taken most seriously.

The planning experiences of many LDCs is to some extent comparable in the sense that planning has often proved largely if not totally ineffective.[27] The French indicative or consultative model, which has had some apparent success in France itself, has been much less effective in those countries – Morocco, Tunisia, Tanzania, Chile – which have sought to import it.[28] Detailed central planning has everywhere, as in India and Turkey, been a distinctly qualified success,[29] as, often, have been more modest efforts at macro-planning with private sector participation (as in Malaysia, Pakistan, Iran and the Philippines).[30] The Korean planning system is perhaps best described as one which seeks to set overall national economic goals and sectoral targets, to achieve them increasingly through conventional macro-economic and budgetary techniques, and, by various means, including consultative processes, to encourage the private sector to enlarge its role in stimulating and directing economic activity. The state's direct role in certain strategic industries, in banking and export assistance remains important.

National planning efforts of all kinds seek heightened rationality in resource mobilization and allocation, efforts which, to have any chance of success, require a complex mix of data, intellectual acumen, skills, organization, stability and social and political acceptance -- resources which are chronically in short supply in many LDCs. The basic tools for LDC planning have been provided, first, by the development of national income accounting, which brought together data and concepts to form variables which could be manipulated by central authorities in their overall direction of economic activity. In some countries, with unrefined statistical approximations, systematic national planning has proved virtually impossible.[31] In the case of Korea, poor statistical quality was by no means the least important obstacle to development in the immediate post-Korean War period, nor was the rapid improvement in Korean statistics since that time a minor contributor to the growth patterns discussed earlier. Korea now has a very comprehensive statistical system (including recent improvements in input-output tables and integrated flow-of-funds and national income accounts) the quality of which, by all accounts, is very high.[32] In addition to national income accounting, other developments in the social sciences – analytic statistics, input and output analysis, systems analysis, operations research, decision theory, game theory -- have improved the capacity of national managers to plan economic development. Finally, monetary theory, with its implications for enhancing the ability of national governments to manage central banking and money supply problems, has been indispensable in national planning. Mastery of these aspects of applied economics, not only intellectually but in a practical administrative sense, is essential to any successful planning effort. Again, as we shall see, the technical ability to apply economic theory in national economic decision-making in Korea has in recent years been spread throughout the policy-making system as many highly trained individuals have assumed positions of importance in the economic agencies. Adequate data and technical competence are among the most important of developmental prerequisties and both have been substantially augmented in Korea in the last decade.

Data and skill, however, will not guarantee good planning in the absence of effective organizational arrangements and political support. These, among the most important of non-economic factors in development, are described in later chapters, but, by general agreement have operated very effectively in Korea in recent years.[33]

Caiden and Wildavsky

A review of the planning experiences of a wide variety of countries suggests that, just as the Korean economic performance has deviated from international patterns, so too has the effectiveness of the Korean planning process. Indeed, two serious scholars, having examined the literature on the planning processes in LDCs extensively (some 80 countries, with three-quarters of the world's population) and intensively (through detailed empirical analysis, including elite interviews, involving 12 countries), concluded with the recommendation that "... formal planning should be eliminated and useful work for planners should be found elsewhere."[34] This is harsh medicine and, given the Korean experience, potentially harmful as well, precisely because, by any reasonable measure, Korean planning has worked. Caiden and Wildavsky's counsel is one of despair – they recommend the "abolition of comprehensive multisectoral planning"[35] and efforts to cope with unemployment of planners (unfortunately, "they have not been trained to think small"), perhaps by absorbing them in project analysis in budgeting and finance agencies (although "... microeconomics, project analysis, is not their forte").[36]

What is the source of this deep skepticism towards national planning? The reasons are many, but essentially it is that planners, if given real influence in decision-making, "... tend to become indistinguishable from the environment they were supposed to transform." If kept on the periphery of power, "... the advice they proffer is ignored."[37] The Caiden and Wildavsky study is an important corrective to the innocence imbedded in so much of the planning literature produced by (only some) administrators and scholars and deserves careful attention for that reason. It is flawed, however, in evolving global recommendations from average cases ("Maybe economic growth takes a long time.")[38] instead of the successful ones. Pervasive optimism is replaced with pervasive skepticism when neither attitude is warrented by the full range of available experiences. Before illustrating this point in greater detail as concerns Korea, a closer enumeration of the Caiden and Wildavsky thesis -- granting its applicability to the general case -- will provide a useful backdrop against which to consider the apparently deviant and special planning experience of Korea.

The Korean case will not falsify the Caiden-Wildavsky thesis if their analysis is taken as one of central tendencies. Actually, however, Caiden and Wildavsky endeavor to state a universal proposition: "How could our theory be falsified? New studies could be made that would show markedly different patterns of behavior in planning and budgeting. Contrary to our findings, plans could be shown to be instruments for controlling futures, and budgets, means of implementing them."[39] Again, "Suppose the general explanation does not fit the particular situation; then it is a bad one."[40]

The problems with effective planning in the LDCs include, in the Caiden and Wildavsky analysis, many factors. Poverty is by definition present and is associated with uncertainty (poor data, lack of trained personnel, communications breakdowns, absence of redundancy or back-up systems).[41] Other factors include budgets which are not susceptive to effective management (because of the micro-level prudence but the macro-level imprudence of finance officials to underestimate revenues and overestimate expenditures);

excessive and delaying scrutiny of spending for previously budgeted purposes; earmarked special funds which cannot be channeled to more efficient uses; recurrent expenditures comprising most of the budget which limit the availability of investment funds; capital budgets, which get controlled by separate organizations beyond normal budgetary control; tendencies to equate the capital budget with the development budget, leading to confusion on priorities.[42] The social and political roles of economic decision-makers, it is held, inhibit rational planning as well. Finance officials seek to maintain a surplus, thus foregoing potential benefits; make across-the-board reductions without regard to the particular merits, which are often unknown in any case, of agency plans; establish spending ceilings not on the basis of economic analysis but of the tax fears and expenditure hopes of interest groups, such fixed ceilings then being altered later through political pressure or maintained arbitrarily without regard to the merit of proposals to pierce the ceiling. Budget examiners invoke incremental decision-rules. "Drastic changes aren't possible."[43] Budgets reflect the outcome of old conflicts, and "even if a new regime were to discredit the old, it still must deal with the same social interests that have a stake in the pattern of spending."[44] Rules-of-thumb – e.g., automatically cut requests that are "too high" – are followed; time and expertise are not sufficient for economic analysis; roles of budget examiners (when to advocate, when to criticize) are confused; priorities emerge which are not established by rational analysis, they "... are not self-evident; officials must search for them."[45]

Chief executives, according to Caiden and Wildavsky, are the most influential actors in determining "who gets what" but are themselves unable to concentrate solely on the objectives of any formal plan: demands for growth, equity and regional improvement must be accommodated regardless of the plan's provisions; time is limited and delegation necessary; ministerial bargaining for the chief executive's favor creates inefficient proposals for his approval; leading figures importune him for special dispensations. The chief executive tends to withdraw from budgeting, because "Budgeting tells the man at the top how really poor his country is. That is why budgeting is not likely to be a favorite activity of chief executives."[46] All in all, scarcity, complexity, short time-frames, sunk obligations, alternative goals, special interests and power combine at the central budgeting and political levels to undermine comprehensive planning.

The operating agencies themselves have limited inducements to comply voluntarily with overall plans according to Caiden and Wildavsky. Most are under pressure to expand their programs; most are committed to securing a higher ranking in the schedule of priorities; and none regards exceptional decisions in its own favor as inconsistent with truly rational planning. Consequently, political tactics are pursued to augment agency resources. Estimates are padded and privileged access to the leadership is sought. At the same time, internal interests compete for budgeted funds; planned projects are poorly implemented; project funds go unspent because of endemic bottlenecks. Departmental goals are in conflict (efficiency v. equity) and ranked and organized not through analysis but power.[47]

For all these (and other) reasons, comprehensive planning is sought as a means of achieving heightened rationality in the allocative process, but planning itself, in the Caiden and Wildavsky analysis, cannot work. Data are poor or lacking altogether, but even when available "overwhelm" the planners. "Simplifying assumptions" must be invoked but there are few guides as to what those assumptions should be.[48] Facts and theory are lacking. Trends being unreliable, targets and means must be set by a large dose of intuition, but even this may be unacceptable to the leadership for political reasons. The computational task of the planners is insoluable; projections of internal savings are difficult enough, while export earnings, if any, and foreign capital flows (grants, direct investment, public/private loans) are even more unpredictable. (Of course, this is one important reason why planners are concerned to expand the mix and reduce the concentration of their exports.) Planners tend to be overoptimistic as to how much foreign savings can be mobilized. Plans are tailored to the schemes of foreign aid-granting entities rather than the higher logic of an optimal plan. Investment criteria are not clear; ranking sector priorities is "hard enough," while specific choices in the absence of data on comparative project efficiency are often beyond compelling intellectual justification and -- merit aside -- of political acceptance.

Developing the plan does not insure compliance with it. Operating agencies and monetary authorities must behave consistently but, for the most part, cannot be induced by planners to do so. In mixed systems, moreover, the private sector cannot be effectively controlled, thus leaving a large share of economic activity outside the plan. In generating projects from the agencies, planners must contend with the fact that agency officials lack understanding (their own planning units are inadequate) and information; administrative authority is divided; and planning may be regarded with skepticism, even hostility. In evaluating projects, planners resort to *ad hoc* decision rules (e.g., finish current projects, no new starts) in the absence of formally operational ones. What formal rules do exist often are variously vague or mutually inconsistent. Alternative projects cannot be compared systematically; some are ideas only, others rough drafts, only a few are detailed blue-prints. Too, planners are not experts in all phases of analysis relevant to project appraisal, and comprehensive cost/benefit analysis cannot be conducted.

Perhaps most importantly, support from political elites may be lacking: "It would seem that the planner who can come up with a viable plan should have little trouble in implementing it under an apparently strong, popular, and sympathetic government." But leaders, while willing to use planning to personal political advantage, "...have been unwilling to submit to its constraints."[49] Governments in the LDCs are insecure, unstable and unable to give full attention to development; yet their commitment is vital, although "...little is heard about what it takes or the price that must be paid."[50] In adjusting to these circumstances, planners acquiesce to the pressure system -- plan so that everybody gets something, lengthen time-frames so that today's impossible imperatives become tomorrow's intention, produce pious if abstract and non-operational plans, do not destabilize the existing balance of social interests, become so flexible in meeting current exigencies that the plan loses its transforming impetus.[51] In the face of all these realities, efforts to plan (to be systematic, efficient, coordinated, and rational) cannot succeed.[52] In fact, "If we [Caiden and Wildavsky] were asked to design a mechanism for decisions to maximize every known disability and minimize any possible advantage of poor countries, we could hardly do better than comprehensive, multisectoral planning."[53]

Certainly it is beyond doubt that national planning involves great problems and Caiden and Wildavsky have surely identified many of them. The question remains, however, as to whether they have not indulged the fallacy of the strong case. Uncertainty, scarcity and politics are features of all human affairs but even among poor countries differ widely in their effects on systematic analysis. One has the greatest difficulty in squaring the history of Korean planning and development with their description. There is a tendency in Caiden and Wildavsky's analysis to neglect certain essential aspects of planning and to accept uncritically certain proverbs of administration, especially in budgeting, which might have benefited from more critical attention. Old-fashioned monetary theory has probably been of greater assistance to national planners than any other aid provided by social science but receives very little attention in terms of cross-national management from Caiden and Wildavsky. One wonders if the budgeting and planning failures in LDCs have had their consistent analogues in the monetary field and, if so, in greater or lesser degree and among all developing systems. In the Korean case, monetary policy, following some early blunders, has in recent years been adjusted on a realistic, if sometimes temporarily painful, basis in terms of national objectives and accounts for much of the Korean achievement. On another front, Caiden and Wildavsky deplore the establishment of capital budgets, the removal of certain activities from budgeting control and the earmarking of revenues, all of which reduce the control of budgeting authorities over public resources and thus inhibit a broader consideration of obligations, opportunities and priorities. Actually, the breaking out of some public enterprise activities from general state budgeting can be part of the planning process. Opportunity cost pricing policies in public enterprise may in fact relieve pressure on the conventional budget and allow for the efficient mobilization of investment in areas that can meet market tests. The fact that such pricing policies decentralize decision-making, frustrate administrative corruption and focus management control and responsibility is an added bonus.[54]

It goes without saying that Korean economic decision-making has made its mistakes. Assessments of available capital have sometimes been inaccurate; inefficient plan-implementation has occurred; the currency reform of 1962, which sought to stem inflation and mobilize capital for investment, failed altogether as the currency lost value and confidence declined rather than increased; efforts to halt usurious loans in the countryside backfired as farmers were forced to sell land, crops and livestock at low prices to pay back government loans which were collected too vigorously; interest rates, foreign exchange rates and the money supply were too rigidly maintained in the face of changing circumstances during the 1960s; the means to assist small and medium-sized industry were sometimes inapt; foreign capital, when generated, was not always fully mobilized.[55] But in the main, the Korean planning and policy-making system has improved greatly over the last decade, a fact attested to by any number of American experts who have observed and some cases assisted in that improvement. Their testimony provides an interesting counter-point to the Caiden/Wildavsky analysis.

Adelman's Assessment

The eminent American economist Irma Adelman served as a consultant to the Korean government and played an active role in the formulation of its Second Five-Year Plan (1967-71). The First Five-Year Plan, promulgated in 1962, rested on the military government's recognition that economic development was essential to the country's (and its own) future, but was hindered in its implementation by a lack of political unity in the country (the plan was broadly attacked by academicians, businessmen, and the political opposition), as well as by unfavorable agricultural conditions (poor harvests occurred in 1962 and 1963) and chronic economic constraints (soaring inflation caused by excessive monetary expansion, low savings and investment). The over-optimism contained in the plan was scaled down by a radical lowering in 1964 of planned growth targets and the modified plan was largely ignored as *ad hoc* efforts at economic stabilization were made. These efforts were by and large successful – consisting of exceedingly tough measures to stem inflation by monetary and fiscal restraints; devaluation and import liberalization stimulated exports and the creation of import-substitute industries; opportunity cost pricing policies loosened direct controls and yielded more efficient resource allocations. With reasonable stabilization secured, it became possible to focus policy on growth. Accordingly, the Second Five-Year Plan was formulated in 1965, approved in 1966 and invoked in January, 1967.[56]

The gross achievements during the planning period have already been discussed. The strategy underlying the plan was to secure an equilibrium of supply and demand in all economic sectors and to stipulate growth targets based on savings (internal and foreign) and the availability of foreign exchange. To balance supply and demand, controls were relaxed in both foreign trade and banking as market decision-making was phased in and administrative decision-making reduced.[57] The dimensions of the stabilization reforms undertaken just prior to the introduction of the Second Plan were of a fundamental character rarely taken in LDCs. In May, 1964, the Korean currency was devalued drastically, while exports, expanding at 40 per cent annually, made possible the liberalization of import policy (and reducing the corruption associated with import licensing). This, combined with interest rate reform (interest rates on deposits were doubled), enhanced the generation of savings and mobilization of investment at much higher levels than previously attained. Increased savings reduced the need for the rationing of credit by non-market criteria. Improvements in tax administration produced sharp marginal increases in revenues which then became available for developmental purposes.[58] Backstopping these policy initiatives was a strong and resolute political authority prepared to alter basically whatever equilibrium of interests -- mostly inchoate at best -- existed in Korea in the early and mid-1960s. A disciplined, mobilizationally and innovatively inclined political regime was undoubtedly an essential prerequisite to the planning successes that came with the Second Five-Year Plan. The same successes rebounded to the benefit of the political authorities by enhancing their legitimacy and, in turn, their capacity to sustain and further rationalize planning and development efforts. (More recent aspects of this question are considered later.) It is noteworthy that these qualities are, according to Caiden/Wildavsky, exceedingly rare in the less-developed world.

Effective political leadership and its willingness to invoke sweeping policy changes to achieve stability produced a context within which planning could be attempted. But as we have seen, arguments have been made that, effort aside, the cognitive capacity required for comprehensive planning is in all circumstances too limited to allow planning to succeed. This, however, is to take an overly literal view of what comprehensive planning entails. In the first place, the contributions that broad conceptual schemes and sophisticated methodologies may make to planning should not be underestimated. In the second place, planning itself may involve efforts to decentralize decisions (thus lowering the decision costs of the planning entity) through a variety of mechanisms. In the third place, the capacity to link planning with action may be greater than sometimes supposed.[59]

On the conceptual plane, it is interesting to refer to Adelman's experience in Korea. The Second Plan was approached, conventionally enough, with a two-fold methodology. (1) A macroeconometric model was developed[60] in order to select a realistic growth rate tied to the availability of foreign earnings and internal and foreign savings. (As it happened, a reliable econometric growth model had for some time to await a revision in the quality of the national income accounts -- an achievement previously referred to and which, judging from Caiden and Wildavsky's comprehensive survey, is clearly atypical of LDCs generally.) (2) A 43 x 43 matrix input-output sectoral model (expanded to 53 sectors in the Fourth Plan) was also formulated to set investment levels, to balance supply and demand by sector, to set specific investment programs and as a consistency measure of the econometric growth model.[61] Finally, a mixed integer programming model[62] was formulated subsequent to the invocation of the Second Plan, both for use in the Third Plan and to measure the welfare gains of two import-substitution investment decisions contained in the Second Plan.[63]

The clarification of Korea's planning problems produced by these several models was itself an important benefit. Adelman notes that the models yielded "... an amazing degree of consistency among their policy conclusions."

Consistency was achieved in identifying: (1) constraints on growth (less from savings, more from foreign exchange limitations); (2) comparative sectoral advantage (light manufacturing and low ICOR, high skill-intensive heavy industry); (3) specific meritorious projects (a petrochemical plant, an integrated iron and steel mill); (4) needed remedies to reverse underinvestment in agriculture; (5) the need for greater attention to physical overhead capital; (6) the desirability of restraining monetary expansion; (7) the need for a currency devaluation. Appropriate decisions in these areas, it was projected, would enable the economy to expand at an annual rate of 10 per cent during the planning period.[64]

Actual results were superior to initial expectations. At the conclusion of the plan in 1971, the Korean GNP stood in 1965 prices at 1599.8 billion won compared to the 1168.7 billion won anticipated in the plan. Actual tax revenues in 1965 prices were 213.4 billion won, while planned revenues were only 180.5 billion won. Savings as a proportion of GNP, which had been projected at 19.9 per cent rose to an actual 25.8 per cent (largely because of unexpected foreign savings -- 11.3 per cent of GNP instead of the planned 5.5 per cent).[65] Adelman's testimony on these developments, in view of the Caiden/Wildavsky analysis, is telling and is worth quoting at some length:

> "The South Korean planning experience has been extraordinary in a number of ways -- it offers an important example of the mutual reinforcement of economic and political development .... the gap between planning theory and (as taught in universities throughout the world) the planning procedure utilized in the formulation (of the plan) was much smaller than usual .... Not

Table 4-1

Second Five-Year Plan (1967-71) Projections and Results (billions of 1965 won and percent)

	Second-Plan estimates and projections			Actuals		
	1965	1968	1971	1965	1968	1971
Internal national tax revenues	41.2	84.7	108.3	42.1	107.1 (156.7)	180.5 (355.5)
Tax burden as a percent of GNP	8.8	13.5	14.2	8.6	14.4	15.6
Central general gov't. domestic revenue	66.2	126.8	161.6	67.1	141.5 (206.6)	240.9 (474.5)
GNP	779.4	954.8	1169.7	805.3	1094.5	1599.8
Saving as a percent of GNP		18.5	19.9	13.9	25.3	25.8
Government saving	0.6	3.1	5.8	1.7	6.3	6.0
Private saving	5.5	6.8	8.6	5.8	7.4	8.5
Foreign saving	6.6	8.6	5.5	6.4	11.6	11.3

NOTE : Figures are in 1965 prices and those in parenthesis are in current prices.

SOURCE : Economic Planning Board.

> only were sophisticated econometric input-output and programming models constructed to assist in the formulation of the plan, a number of their results were used in the plan itself .... the administrative and institutional mechanisms for planning and plan implementation were strongly influenced by the formal planning technology, and vice versa ... the planning process led to a vast improvement in the country's data base, which, in turn, led to improved planning models. Last, but not least, the plan appears to be successful .... very high growth ... has been maintained, the rate of inflation has decreased, and bottlenecks that were anticipated before the plan was adopted have been much less severe than one would have expected in the absence of planning .. The entire effort was achieved with a handful of young, energetic governmental officials and a small group of Korean academicians and foreign advisors as prime movers."[66]

Brown's Assessment

It is worth noting parenthetically that the First Five-Year Plan (1962-66), although failing to meet most of its objectives,[67] did contain suggestions that were contained in the Second Plan, most importantly in the area of pricing policies. These policies advanced the view that resources for investment in state owned or controlled enterprises -- railroads, communications, electricity -- should be mobilized by the enterprises themselves on the basis of opportunity cost (or simulated market mechanism) pricing.[68] The proposed reduction in unproductive subsidies derived from essentially the same argument. This relatively early recognition that the market mechanism could be a powerful planning tool, and was not necessarily the same thing as private enterprise, is a lesson still to be learned in many planning quarters. Hirschman, Lindblom, Stolper, Brown, and others have made the case for the potential significance of this dissociation.[69] The Korean policy movement towards the profitability criterion that began with the First Plan and has continued to the present is not a conventional one among other LDCs. It grew from awareness among a small group of Korean economists that, having exhausted the possibilities of import-substitution schemes and faced with the problems which such schemes involve (unrealistic exchange rates; cumbersome and rigorous controls on imports and capital allocations; artificial interest rates; inefficient and low-saving state enterprises; the corruption and administrative problems involved in managing these decisions), policies designed to increase efficiency, expand exports and generate foreign savings would have to rely much more extensively on market mechanisms. The aptness of this policy reorientation has been demonstrated by history; in the policy/planning arena it was this departure that set Korea apart from the policy choices of most other LDCs.

De-centralization of choices through market mechanisms seeks to tap developmental energies by offering concrete material inducements to individuals, fiduciaries and managers both at home and abroad. The market, actual or simulated through shadow pricing, organizes activity through the signals and incentives of the price system (prices, their movements, their differentials, and income flows) rather than through administrative proscription. Much of planning in Korea has consisted in planning the manner in which market mechanisms could be used to achieve social goals and to vastly simplify administrative burdens while doing so. Viewing markets as instruments of developmental planning, Lindblom notes, "...represents a revolution in practical economic thought and in the understanding of possibilities of plan administration. The new view has not encompassed the world -- and is either unnoticed or resisted in some nations ... [a fact] in some part attributable to the influence of turn-of-the-century socialist thought on the intellectual and administrative traditions of some of the new or newly freed developing nations."[70] This intellectual stricture was one tribulation from which Korea has not had to free itself and its absence may well be an important factor in the uncommon success of Korean planning. Korean administrators and economists, by all accounts, are a pragmatic, non-ideological class much more interested in the concrete serviceability of their resources and skills than in loyalty to a generally failed ideological paradigm. Openness to alternative approaches and receptiveness to innovations have characterized the Korean planning approach from its beginnings.[71]

Planning the market mechanism does not by any means suggest that all centralized public choices can be avoided. The planning of a more acceptable income distribution remains an important activity; direct investments and/or allocations in/to merit and public goods and services should properly continue at appropriate levels; stabilization objectives must be secured; the efficiency of markets requires oversight and coordination; continual judgmental effort to approximate "correct" (shadow price or competitive market equilibrium) pricing levels in, e.g., exchange rates, interest rates, state and private enterprise monopolies, is essential.

Brown's exhaustive treatment of pricing policies makes a strong case for the efficacy of these policies in Korean development. In sector after sector (fiscal policy and government saving; government product pricing; agricultural pricing and marketing, exchange rates and trade policies; interest rates and domestic saving; foreign credit flows; stabilization and monetary policy), Brown concludes, the policy shift to equilibrium pricing (the profitability criterion) "released the potential for achievement that previously was frustrated and dissipated by alternative policies."[72] Brown's assessment of the primacy of the policy shift is interesting: "While the rapidity of Korean growth during the 1960s cannot be fully explained apart from the historical-political-cultural-economic base on which it was built, neither can it be explained primarily on that basis."[73] Brown, like Adelman, is effusive in his praise of Korea's Second Five-Year Plan and its implementation. He notes that the Plan, unlike the multi-year plans of so many LDCs, paid major attention to the monetary-fiscal-exchange rates and trade policy dimensions of planning (a subject curiously neglected in the Caiden/Wildavsky study of LDC plans), an aspect of planning fully as important as investments.[74] Finally, it should be noted that the profitability criterion has not been applied dogmatically. The inflationary energy crisis of 1973-74 induced the government to repress price increases of the public utilities, particulary the railroads, in an effort to mitigate effects on consumer prices. Step by step increases were then permitted in 1975-77 in a gradual return to general policy.

Success with the Second Plan laid the basis for the goals of the Third. The Third Plan, concluded in 1976, called, among other things, for the rapid development of the rural economy, an objective realized in 1976 when rural/urban incomes were equalized and had risen to nearly $700 per capita annually, or about $80 more than anticipated in the Plan. Parity in rural/urban incomes, a milestone in development, promised to reduce urban migration, increase investment in the countryside and contribute to balanced regional development. Increased agricultural productivity leading to self-sufficiency in major food grains was also an important objective of the Third Plan. Improvements in irrigation, rice paddy alignment, mechanization and multiple-purpose river basin development were the major physical programs for achieving self-sufficiency. By 1976, Korea was, for the first time in decades, self-sufficient in rice, although it was still necessary to purchase some food grains from abroad. The third major goal of the Plan ("a dramatic and sustained increase in exports") was secured as well.

The Third Plan called for Korea's share of exports in world trade to grow from 0.3 per cent to 0.8 per cent in 1976, a target precisely reached. Annual export growth was very high during the planning period (80 per cent in 1973, 45 per cent in 1974, 15 per cent in 1975 and 45 per cent in 1976) and exports in 1976 reached $7.8 billion, exceeding the objective for that year by $3.52 billion.

The final major goal of the Third Plan – the establishment of heavy and chemical industries -- was also vigorously pursued. Growth in manufacturing expanded at an annual rate of over 18 per cent, and in heavy and chemical industries by over 23 per cent. The share of heavy and chemical exports in total exports reached 30 per cent in 1976, compared to 2 per cent in the early 1960s.

The capacity to support the ambitious goals of the Fourth Plan (see Chapter 6) was strengthened and stabilized

Table 4-2

Manufacturing Production in Korea

	1962	1975
Iron and steel	.14 mill.	2.61 mill. M/T
Shipbuilding	5,000	819,000 G/T
Fertilizer production	37,000	880,000 M/T
Cement production	.79 mill.	10.13 mill. M/T
Automobiles	0	36,000 units
Power tillers	0	34,437 units
Mixed woolen fabrics	.4 mill.	13.4 mill. M^2
Plywood	217,000	1,854,000 M^2

during 1972-76. Internal tax revenues, while initially lagging behind the Third Plan's projections, rose rapidly toward the end of the planning period to exceed expectations by a substantial margin. Increased administrative efficiency, a high rate of economic activity, and adjusted tax rates were responsible. Government savings were less than called for in the Plan (5.3 per cent of GNP in 1976 instead of the planned 7.5 per cent), but enlarged private and foreign savings meant that total savings (24.7 per cent of GNP in 1976) approached the plan's objectives. (See Table 4-3.)

Table 4-3

Third Five-Year Plan (1972-76) Projections and Results (billions of won and percent)

	Third-Plan Projections			Currently Estimated Actuals		
	1972	1974	1976	1972	1974	1976
Internal national tax revenues	375.6	444.3	528.1	294.7 (374.3)	405.6 (718.0)	541.3 (1347.8)
Tax burden as percent of GNP	12.3	12.3	12.4	13.5	15.1	19.0
Central general gov't domestic revenue	497.7	592.8	707.8	474.1 (602.1)	570.6 (1010.0)	848.1 (2113.2)
GNP	3071.8	3616.2	4257.1	3039.4 (3860.0)	3830.0 (6779.1)	4697.0 (11695.5)
Savings as % of GNP	25.3	24.6	24.9	20.6	32.7	24.7
Government savings	7.5	7.6	7.5	3.9	3.0	5.3
Private savings	10.2	11.8	14.0	11.1	16.2	15.3
Foreign savings	7.6	5.2	3.4	5.6	13.5	4.1

NOTE : Figures are in 1970 constant prices and those in parenthesis are in current prices.

SOURCE : Economic Planning Board.

Summary

The type of authoritative choices associated with national planning and decision-making – public choices – cannot, for both formal and practical reasons, be evaluated unambiguously in terms of either the economist's social welfare function or the political scientist's varied concepts of the public interest. It is not possible to order public choices by processes similar to those through which the optimal allocation of private goods and services under precisely stated market conditions becomes theoretically possible. The characteristics of public goods, the nature of non-market interdependencies, the imperfect mechanisms for aggregating individual preferences, public responsibility to future generations, and pervasive uncertainty combine to suggest that public choices must be evaluated often with other criteria, namely, the extent to which government's grant of authority and discretion is responsibly managed. Disagreement on such questions (the classical questions of both economics and political science) is likely. The Korean government's ranking of goals (security, development) appears to be broadly if not uniformly supported throughout the society.

National planning, as a means to the rapid achievement of developmental goals, has often failed in the LDCs for practical reasons as well, as shown in Caiden and Wildavsky's analysis. The reasons for such failures include the weakness and contradictory goals of the political leadership, inadequate data and consequent uncertainty, bureaucratic infighting, the absence of resources, inadequate technical competence, planning entities that are either on the edge of power or absorbed by the environment they exist to transform. The Korean planning experience deviates significantly from the apparent norm, however. Leadership support for planning decisions has been forthcoming since the early 1960s; planning data were radically improved; technical competence of a very high order was developed on the planning staffs; resources for developmental objectives were secured once economic stabilization and political order were established; major attention was paid to important matters often neglected in LDC planning (e.g., monetary, pricing, and trade policy); flexibility was maintained while objectives (growth) remained constant. The Second Five-Year Plan (1967-71), by common acknowledgment, was a success by any reasonable standard. The Third Plan (1972-76) was equally successful. There can be little doubt that the public policies derived from the planning function in Korea were indispensable to the economic growth of the last 10-15 years, or that the market mechanism as a tool of planning has yielded economic improvements which, against the social backdrop of the early 1960s, have been altogether extraordinary.

The political and administrative means by which the planning process has been rendered unusually effective in Korea and the more recent direction and consequences of Korean planning are subjects taken up in the following chapters.

Notes

1. See the perceptive treatment of this question in Sung-Joo Han, *The Failure of Democracy in South Korea* (Berkeley: University of California Press, 1974).

2. For example, from Gregory Henderson, in his review of Han's study in *Journal of Asian Studies,* Vol. XXIV (February, 1975), pp. 531-33.

3. Most notably by Gilbert T. Brown, *Korean Pricing Policies and Economic Development in the 1960s* (Baltimore: The Johns Hopkins University Press, 1973), and, from a more political perspective, by David C. Cole and Princeton N. Lyman, *Korean Development: The Interplay of Politics and Economics* (Cambridge: Harvard University Press, 1971). Also see Irma Adelman (ed.), *Practical Approaches to Development Planning: Korea's Second Five-Year Plan* (Baltimore: The Johns Hopkins University Press, 1969).

4. Hahn-Been Lee, *Korea: Time, Change and Administration* (Honolulu: East-West Center Press, 1968) examines the transformation in attitudes that occurred in the modern Korean policy system which led to less discounting of the future by political and administrative decision-makers. Very large increases in investment followed.

5. The theory of public goods, which began with the classical economists, is given historical context in William J. Baumal, *Welfare Economics and the Theory of The State* (Cambridge: Harvard University Press, 1952), and received its modern impetus by Paul A. Samuelson, "The Pure Theory of Public Expenditures," *Review of Economics and Statistics* XXXVI (November, 1954), pp. 387-389. An innovative treatment of the subject is James M. Buchanan, *The Demand and Supply of Public Goods* (Chicago: Rand McNally, 1968).

6. There is one institution -- unanimity in voting – which would allow the costs and benefits of public goods to be allocated efficiently when decision costs are ignored. Such a system would provide a public analogue to the free market but is rarely relied upon in practice because of the decision costs involved and because, in diverse populations, no decision would ever be taken. This, the so-called Wicksellian proposal, functions analytically to reveal the practical impossibility of Pareto optimal choices by governments, which must adopt other than unanimity decision rules. See Buchanan, *The Demand and Supply of Public Goods,* pp. 1-10.

7. Not only will diversity of preferences and unacceptable decision costs make the unanimity rule impractical, any less inclusive rule, say simple majority rule, may involve (in addition to the losses sustained by

the minority) intransitive collective preferences of the sort associated with the now famous voting paradox analyzed in its modern form by Kenneth Arrow in *Social Choice and Individual Values* (New York: Wiley, 1951). The reluctance of many political scientists to face up to the implications of these matters for democratic theory is a most interesting phenomenon.

8. The fact that all decision rules are two-edged and sources of danger as well as protection is one way of understanding democratic constitutions. See James M. Buchanan and Gordon Tullock, *The Calculus of Consent: Logical Foundations of Constitutional Democracy* (Ann Arbor: University of Michigan Press, 1962).

9. The best-known and most influential of these is Anthony Downs, *An Economic Theory of Democracy* (New York: Harper & Row, 1957). Another suggestive work is William Niskanen, *Representative Government and Bureaucracy* (Chicago: Aldine, 1971).

10. See Richard Zeckhauser, "Voting Systems, Honest Preferences and Pareto Optimality," *American Political Science Review,* Vol. LXVII (September, 1973), pp. 934-46.

11. On the problem of interpersonal comparisons in welfare economics, see I.M.D. Little, *A Critique of Welfare Economics* (London: Oxford University Press, 1958). On intransitive social rankings, see Arrow, *Social Choice and Individual Values.*

12. For informed discussions of the public interest concept, see Richard E. Flathman, *The Public Interest* (New York: Wiley, 1966); and Glendon Schubert, *The Public Interest* (New York: The Free Press, 1960).

13. Flathman, *The Public Interest,* p. 6.

14. Schubert, *The Public Interest,* p. 11.

15. *Ibid.*, p. 31.

16. Perhaps the most successful effort by a political scientist to "solve" the problem of aggregation of individual preferences by methods of both majority rule and bargaining (minority opportunities) is Robert A Dahl's *Preface to Democratic Theory* (Chicago: University of Chicago Press, 1956). However useful Dahl's analysis may be, it is not particularly relevant to what may be the world's most homogeneous country. The relative absence of social differentiation in Korea along racial, religious, regional, linguistic or traditional class lines provides the organizing dimension to Gregory Henderson's *Korea: The Politics of the Vortex* (Cambridge: Harvard University Press, 1968).

17. The test of "fairness" in policy making and evaluation developed in John Rawls' influential *A Theory of Justice* (Cambridge: Harvard University Press, 1971), which suggests that no policy should damage the weaker members of society, has been shown to be less than helpful in many and important concrete cases and to yield absurd decisions in others. See John C. Harsanyi, "Can the Maximin Principle Serve as a Basis for Morality? A Critique of John Rawls' Theory, "*American Political Science Review*, Vol. LXIX (June, 1975), pp. 594-606.

18. See Jerome Rothenberg, *The Measurement of Social Welfare* (Engelwood Cliffs, N.J.: Prentice-Hall, 1961).

19. For further elaboration, see Simon Kuznets, *Population, Capital, and Growth* (New York: Norton, 1973), pp. 121-164.

20. *Ibid.*, pp. 132-33.

21. See Alec Nove, "The Problem of Success Indicators in Soviet Industry," *Economica*, 25 (February, 1958), pp. 1-13.

22. Dwight H. Perkins, "Plans and Their Implementation in the People's Republic of China," *Papers and Proceedings of the 85th Annual Meeting* of the American Economic Association (May, 1973), pp. 224-231.

23. E. Wheelwright and B. McFarlane, *The Chinese Road to Socialism* (New York: Monthly Review Press, 1970).

24. Perkins, "Plans and Their Implementation in the People's Republic of China," p. 228.

25. *Ibid.*, pp. 228-29.

26. See the discussion by Alec Nove, "Market Socialism and Its Critics," *Soviet Studies*, 25 (July, 1972), pp. 120-37; and N. Fedorenko, "Prices and Optimal Planning," *Problems of Economics,* 10 (November, 1967), pp. 11-21.

27. The most comprehensive analysis of planning results in LDCs is by Naomi Caiden and Aaron Wildavsky, *Planning and Budgeting in Poor Countries* (New York: Wiley, 1974). Also see Albert Waterston, *Development Planning* (Baltimore: The Johns Hopkins University Press, 1965).

28. See John C. Honey, *Planning and The Private Sector* (New York: Dunellen, 1970). On the French experience, see P. Bauchet, *Economic Planning* (New York: Praeger, 1964). On types and objectives of plans, see Michael P. Todard, *Development Planning* (Nairobi: Oxford, 1971), Chapter 1.

29. Honey, *Planning and The Private Sector,* pp. 13-24.

30. *Ibid.*, pp. 25-50.

31. See Wolfgang Stolper, *Planning Without Facts* (Cambridge: Harvard University Press, 1966).

32. See Gilbert T. Brown, *Korean Pricing Policies,* pp. 282-86; and Irma Adelman, "Introduction," pp. 3-10.

33. Adelman, "Introduction." On the importance of the political leadership's commitment to development, see Irma Adelman and C. T. Morris, *Society, Politics and Economic Development: A Quantitative Approach* (Baltimore: The Johns Hopkins University, 1967).

34. Caiden and Wildavsky, *Planning and Budgeting in Poor Countries,* p. X.

35. *Ibid.*, p. 294.

36. *Ibid.*, p. 295.

37. *Ibid.*

38. *Ibid.*, p. 322.

39. *Ibid.*, p. XV.

40. *Ibid.*, p. XVII.

41. *Ibid.*, pp. 45-63.

42. *Ibid.*, pp. 66-97.

43. *Ibid.*, p. 106.

44. *Ibid.*

45. *Ibid., p. 114.*

46. *Ibid.*, p. 124, pp. 101-125.

47. *Ibid.*, pp. 137-165.

48. *Ibid.*, p. 176.

49. *Ibid.*, p. 196.

50. *Ibid.*, p. 200.

51. *Ibid.*, pp. 167-238.

52. *Ibid.*, p. 293.

53. *Ibid.*, pp. 275-291. Caiden and Wildavsky's reform proposals, centering on budgeting, are developed in pp. 293-322.

54. These subjects are explored at length in Gilbert T. Brown, *Korean Pricing Policies*.

55. Mistakes in these areas are cited by President Park Chung Hee in *To Build a Nation* (Washington, D.C.: Acropolis Books, 1971), pp. 123-124.

56. Adelman, "Introduction," p. 4-5. It is worth considering whether stabilization is a prior condition for successful planning in LDCs; the Korean case suggests as much. Unfortunately, this question is not addressed in the Caiden/Wildavsky study. The assessment of the Second Five-Year Plan by Cole and Lyman, *Korean Development*, pp. 216-21 is similar to Adelman's and need not be separately discussed, except to note that the consistency of observation strengthen Adelman's (and Brown's) conclusions.

57. *Ibid.*, p. 5.

58. *Ibid.*, pp. 5-6.

59. Two volumes in which the possibilities of comprehensive planning are questioned are Charles E. Lindblom, *The Intelligence of Democracy* (New York: Macmillan, 1964), and more recently by the same author, *The Policy-Making Process* (Englewood Cliffs, N.J.: Prentice Hall, 1968). Also see J. A. Mirrlees and N. H. Stern, "Fairly Good Plans," *Journal of Economic Theory*, Vol. 4 (April, 1972), pp. 268-88.

60. The model is published in Irma Adelman and Kim Mahn Je, "An Econometric Model of the Korean Economy (1956-66)," in Adelman, *Practical Approaches to Development Planning*, pp. 77-108. On macroeconometric forecasting generally, see Jacob Minzer, *Economic Forecasting and Expectations*, (New York: Columbia University Press 1969).

61. See Irma Adelman, David C. Cole, Roger Morton and Lee Kee Jung, "The Korean Sectoral Model," in *Ibid.*, pp. 109-143. The fact that the original Korean analysis went through many revisions, all without computer assistance, is interesting testimony to the rapidly improving competence of the Korean planners during the 1960s. Trial and error

techniques may be attributes of rational planning, as shown in Michael Kenen, "On The Tautness of Plans," *Review of Economic Studies,* Vol. 39 (October, 1972), pp. 469-86; and Charles Hillinger, "The Design of Economic Policy – or Learning by Doing," *Journal of Economic Issues*, Vol. 4 (December, 1970), pp. 90-93.

62. Larry E. Westphal, "Multisectoral Project Analysis Employing Mixed Integer Programming," in Adelman, *Practical Approaches to Development*, pp. 145-183. Mixed integer programming seeks to consider simultaneously a range of investment alternatives and arrive at a general-equilibrium solution for investment when effects from economies of scale and industrial interdependencies are present. The purpose is to replace cost/benefit analysis of individual projects with a dynamic, multisectoral optimizing analysis for investments with the greatest welfare gains.

63. Adelman, "Introduction," p. 7.

64. *Ibid.*, pp. 7-8.

65. Brown, *Korean Pricing Policies*, p. 59.

66. Adelman, "Introduction," pp. 9-10.

67. Major projected and actual results are available in Brown, *Korean Pricing Policies*, p. 54.

68. Economic Planning Board, *Complementary Plan of The First Five Year Economic Development Plan* (February, 1964).

69. See Otto O. Hirschman, *The Strategy of Economic Development* (New Haven: Yale University Press, 1958); Charles E. Lindblom, "Economics and the Administration of National Planning," *Public Administration Review,* Vol. 25 (December, 1965), pp. 244-283; Stolper, *Planning Without Facts;* Benjamin Cohen and Gustav Ranis, "The Second Post-War Restructuring," in Gustav Ranis (ed.), *Government and Economic Development* (New Haven: Yale University Press, 1971); Brown, *Korean Pricing Policies;* and C. J. Bliss, "Prices, Markets and Planning," *Economic Journal*, Vol. 82 (March, 1972), pp. 87-100.

70. Lindblom, "Economics and the Administration of National Planning," p. 282.

71. The impact of ideology on bureaucratic innovation in the LDCs is a vital

but unchartered subject. A study of public sector innovation in developed systems (the American states) by George W. Downs, Jr., *Bureaucracy, Innovation and Public Policy* (Boston: Lexington-Heath, 1977), could provide the foundation for remedying this gap. It appears that ideologically committed planners in the LDCs often redouble fidelity to their failed planning schemes rather than reassess the viability of their commitments. Since their plans have not generated development (see Caiden and Wildavsky), their goals may shift from growth to equity (thereby achieving neither) as a means of reducing the dissonance between ideology and results. Korean planners radically altered their schemes in the early 1960s without changing their goals (rapid growth) and achieved growth *and* relative equity as a result.

72. Brown, *Korean Pricing Policies*, p. 268.

73. *Ibid.*, pp. 267-68.

74. *Ibid.*, pp. 251, 251-263. The potential of monetary policy as a developmental aid is discussed (an extensive bibliography is also included) by Yung Chul Park, "The Role of Money in Stabilization Policy in Developing Countries," *International Monetary Fund Staff Papers*, Vol. 20 (1973), pp. 379-418.

Chapter 5

Decision Rules and Economic Policy in Korea

In the literature of contemporary political science, the importance of political systems and institutions in the making of public and social choices is often minimized for both theoretical and empirical reasons. At the theoretical level, Marxists (for well-known reasons) and non-Marxists (for different reasons) alike have tended to regard a political institution focus as leading one to arid legal formalisms and away from the dynamic, informal, value-laden relationships and more "basic" structural imperatives which, properly understood, yield greater insights into politics and the policy-making process.[1] On the empirical plane, studies have been published in recent years which, with similar import and not without challenge, seek to show that political variables have considerably less weight in the making of public policy than other environmental (usually economic) factors such as per capita income, level of urbanization, industrialization and so forth.[2] These conclusions, emerging for the most part from studies of the American states, have in some few cases also been extended to include cross-national policy outcomes;[3] these have also been vigorously challenged.[4]

Obviously, non-political factors set limits, both minima and maxima, upon what a nation is able to achieve in the way of policy dispensations. For example, only with its Fourth Five-Year Plan (1977-81) has Korea been able to lay stress upon social welfare, resources for such concerns having been mobilized only recently. Moreover, culture, which stipulates values for a society, may influence public policy in ways irrespective of that society's political forms. In point of fact, it is quite foolish to settle upon any unidimensional explanation of the policy process: societies are complex, and public policy emerges from the interplay of cultural values, available resources, the organization of power, and the structures and processes of political institutions. An explanation of Korean development will require the collaborative effort, therefore, of sociologists, anthropologists, psychologists, political scientists, economists and historians, and it is even then likely that no explanation will be forthcoming in which all contributing factors are precisely weighted and integrated into an unarguable theoretical statement. Korean development is no miracle but some measure of its mystery will remain to intrigue future scholars. But whatever else may be true, the public institutions and public men associated with Korean development must, in any event, figure prominently in explaining it, and are, together with certain related cultural factors, the subjects of the remainder of this chapter. The changing machinery of the Korean governmental system and its emerging stability and institutionalization provided the basis for effective long-range planning, orderly policy implementation and international investors' confidence. The chronic instability of the post-World War II period was overcome and domestic and international resources (both physical and psychological) mobilized by an increasingly effective and capable governmental apparatus. Political institutions are undeniably important; they are, as Swerdlow puts it, "...influential, standard-setting, noticed and valued by their environment and essential to society's operation."[5] The transformation and enhanced capabilities of the Korean government realized since the establishment of the First Republic in 1948 are traced below.

The First Republic

The first Constitution of the Republic of Korea was promulgated on July 17, 1948 after three years of U.S. Military Government. Although the government was ostensibly modeled on the presidential system of the United States, it was actually a fusion of the American model with the European cabinet system. Initially, the drafters of the Constitution had proposed a two-chamber and parliamentary cabinet system. This was on the grounds that the scheme entailed political instability and administrative inefficiency. Consequently, the Constitution was designed as a hybrid of the presidential and parliamentary systems, and embodied, among other things: (1) the indirect election of the President and Vice-President by a single-chamber Assembly; (2) the right of the National Assembly to approve the appointment of the Prime Minister; (3) the right of the Prime Minister and members of the State Council (cabinet) to hold concurrent membership in the National Assembly; (4) cabinet responsibility through a counter-signature system; and (5) the right of the government to submit legislative bills to the National Assembly.[6]

In mid-1952, a constitutional amendment adopting the direct presidential election system passed the National Assembly and other legal requirements as a result of efforts by the ruling party to enable Syngman Rhee to maintain power, there being every indication that, because of the numerical inferiority of the ruling party in the Assembly, Rhee would not be reelected. There was no change in ruling personalities as a result of the amendment, but the new decision-rule did significantly reinforce both the presidential system and Rhee's power.

As the termination of Syngman Rhee's second term

approached, the ruling Liberal Party sought a second amendment to the Constitution in an effort to continue Rhee's presidency. The amendment bill was passed by the ruling party through adoption of a questionable voting rule ("rounding off to the nearest integer") and another important element of the cabinet system was removed, bringing the Korean government still closer to the presidential model. Specifically, the premiership system and the provision for a vote of no-confidence in the State Council were abolished, together with the requirement of joint responsibility of the State Council to the National Assembly.

The Second Republic

The student uprising of April, 1960 and the termination of the Rhee government were described in Chapter 1. The immediate response of the newly dominant political circles to the fall of Rhee was to seek a new and democratic constitutional system to check the rise of arbitrary power in the future. These concerns focused legally on amending the Constitution and adopting a parliamentary government. In the political atmosphere of the time, the cabinet system was deemed, universally if uncritically, as the only curative for the maladministration which characterized the late Rhee period. In the passions of the moment, any antagonism toward installing the parliamentary system was regarded as defiling the spirit of April 19th and tarnishing the sacrifices of the revolutionary young students. In these unsettled circumstances, the Constitution of the Second Republic (third revision) passed the National Assembly on June 24,1960 and adopted the classic cabinet and two-chamber system. With the new Constitution, the Prime Minister could exercise strong power as *primus inter pares* in the cabinet.

The Third Republic

The constitutional function was suspended temporarily between May 16, 1961, when the military revolution took place, and December 17, 1963, when the Third Republic was born. During this period of two years and seven months, the Supreme Council for National Reconstruction acted as the ultimate public authority. The Supreme Council was composed of twenty to thirty or so military personnel on active duty who had taken part in the revolution and who took full control over administration, legislation and adjudication. The Cabinet and the Central Intelligence Agency were established as the executive organ and central security entity respectively under the Supreme Council. The Constitution of the Third Republic (the fifth revision) was adopted by national referendum on December 26, 1962.[7]

The Constitution of the Third Republic was characterized by a formally perfected presidential executive and a one-chamber legislative system. Special emphasis was thus given to the establishment of governmental stability through the strengthening of presidential authority. The Constitution provided for presidential appointment of the Prime Minister without Assembly sanction and for a Cabinet with only deliberative and not legislative powers to assist the President in administrative management. Advisory organs such as the Economic-Science Council and National Security Council were also organized under direct presidential control. The Constitution of the Third Republic thus was in striking contrast to that of the First Republic, which had embodied the premiership and cabinet systems to curtail presidential authority.

The one-chamber system was adopted, actually or

ostensibly, in the interests of efficiency. Additionally, a Political Party Law was instituted, prohibiting independent candidacies for the Assembly and stipulating the legally required minimum number of district chapters of political parties. Together with the elimination of the proportional representation electoral system, the effect was to reduce the traditional hyper-factionalism of Korean party politics and, at the same time, the power of the National Assembly.[8] The Act thus contained a trade-off between legislative independence and increased political order and coherence. A consequence for party politics was the effective consolidation of party opposition into a single party, the New Democratic Party.

The Fourth Republic

Changes in the domestic and international environments in the 1970s brought further trials to the constitutional system of Korea. In response, President Park Chung Hee mandated a "revitalizing" reform, or Yushin system, acting under a nationwide emergency martial law on October 17, 1972, and took supraconstitutional emergency measures that resulted in another temporary suspension of constitutional government. Ten days later, the seventh revision of the Constitution[9] was announced by an emergency Cabinet Council and adopted by a national referendum conducted in November, 1972. This revised Constitution came into effect in December and thus formally inaugurated the Fourth Republic.

The formal organization of the Fourth Republic embodies, first, the National Conference for Unification. This Conference, with the Chief Executive as its chairman, is composed of 2,000-5,000 representatives with six-year terms of office. The constitutional functions of the Conference are to deliberate on unification policies, elect the President and one-third of the members of the National Assembly recommended by the Chief Executive, and decide upon amendments to the Constitution.

Under the 1972 Yushin reforms, the President is empowered to exercise much more authority than in preceeding constitutional regimes. For example, the presidential tenure of office is extended to six years under the Yushin system, the President is elected indirectly by the National Conference for Unification, and may hold consecutive terms without restriction. In addition, the president is also empowered to dissolve the National Assembly if necessary. Furthermore, he exercises authority to take emergency measures that require neither the consent nor the judicial examination of the National Assembly and to appoint the judiciary, including the President of the Supreme Court. The Prime Minister and Cabinet Council perform advisory and administrative functions but have limited constitutional authority.[10]

The authority that can be exercised by the National Assembly over the executive consists at most in potentially dismissing the Prime Minister and Cabinet members and demanding their presence and answers in the National Assembly. Even in a case of their failure to comply with a demand of the National Assembly, there exists no legal right to force them to appear. It is also worthy of mention that the National Assembly now lacks its one-time authority to inspect government offices for oversight purposes.

The important conclusion one can draw from the history of the evolution of Korean political institutions is that earlier regimes were founded on the belief that

Western-style liberal democracy was appropriate to and workable within the Korean context. Basic to this view was the notion that such a democratic system should involve the separation or balancing of legislative, executive and judicial powers. If history is the best judge of these matters, such conceptions have been shown to be erroneous. Based as they were on the assumption that Anglo-American political norms, practices and institutions, then altogether foreign to Korean society, could be made to work effectively in a radically different cultural, economic and historical environment, the result was political cynicism and instability rather than harmony, liberty and order. Contrary to these ideals, political and other realities in Korea were uncongenial to the transplantation of foreign institutions. Traditional Korea had been characterized by an ancient royal ascendency; illiteracy in the early post-war years was high; the country was agricultural; the people poor. The persistent gap between political idealism and social reality remained one of the sources of political irrationality and instability in Korea.

Thus, except for the short-lived Chang Myon regime, all successive regimes moved to increasingly stronger versions of the presidential system. With every constitutional change, power was further consolidated in the presidency, together with the expansion and/or reinforcement of administrative power. As a matter of fact, in the long history of Korea only Chang's regime had adopted a formal plural system. And it was arguably an inevitable consequence that such a system produced disorder and confusion in a society where no firm tradition of liberal democratic politics existed. Be that as it may, Korean society today is directed by a consolidated administration-oriented government in which the goals of national security and economic development share priority with efforts to create a unique and indigenous if yet unspecified political order based on local values and imperatives. Consequently, it is evolving toward a still vague political form that will surely be quite different from Anglo-American political liberalism. With the increase in executive power, the role of administrative organizations in policy formation has been enlarged as well.

Korean Administrative Structure

Administrative structure in government usually refers to the bureaucratic organization of the executive. Such a limited usage may inadvertently lay too much emphasis on the importance of the formal machinery of government and lead to its unwarranted ascendancy, the abuse of administrative power, excessive concern with bureaucratic prerogatives, and a tendency to make much of the government and little of the people. Administrative structure might be better understood in a broad sense to refer to the avenues through which public policy is made and implemented. The administrative structure in this sense consists of two channels, one of which is the self-governing administrative structure and the other is the mandatory or official administrative structure. Below, we discuss the Korean administrative structure as it concerns these two channels.

Voluntary Administrative Structure

When policy implementation is understood to imply the materialization of substantial change in the established living patterns and attitudes of a people, the significance of a self-governing administrative structure may be readily grasped. If the Seoul Municipal Government wishes to install a one-way traffic system on certain streets, it is necessary to change the habitual routines of drivers and pedestrians. In this case the collective body that produces the requisite change of attitude and behavior may be regarded as the administrative structure. In view of the fact that unofficial groups and individuals play roles as crucial to the plan's success as traffic policemen (the bureaucracy), they are the members of the administrative structure. In addition, other typical constituents of self-governing administrative structures might be mentioned: e.g., parents and teachers of private schools participating in the implementation of national policy for compulsory education; middle and high school teachers engaging in the street campaign for a "quiet Christmas"; the Korean Press and Broadcasting Ethics Committees, Korean Businessmen's Association, etc., participating in government-sponsored juvenile guidance programs.

In the case of Korea, where the custom of putting bureaucratic officials above the people still often prevails, it is important to analyze the great contribution that expansions in self-governing administrative structures could make to development. The absence of such structures compels officials to bear excessively heavy decision and implementation costs, while affected citizens become suspicious of policy handed down from above and consequently recalcitrant in their response. The Saemaul (New Community) Movement is a grand experiment to alter this pattern and to involve the people in choice-making and administration and, as such, has been broadly successful. Still, many decisions have been implemented under the initiative of administrative officials and not from the voluntary participation of impacted citizens. Significant opportunities for increases in self-administration thus exist in Korea, some of which are now being explored. It is not too much to say that the next phase of Korean development must involve a large expansion in the participation by the population in policy administration. As the Saemaul Movement is extended to the cities, popular participation in maintaining and enhancing the commons -- baths, streets, neighborhoods, public transportation -- should produce more attractive environments, civic pride, less pressure on the formal administrative system and greater trust and confidence of the population in public institutions.

Mandatory Administrative Structure

The term mandatory administrative structure refers to the formal channel of policy choice and implementation. Included generally in this channel are courts, elected officials, advisory committees, bureaucracy, and the like.

The laws and rules which are characteristic of a modern nation empower the courts to oversee the public policy process. From this point of view, the judiciary is an integral part of the administrative structure. Under the Yushin Constitution, the President is empowered to appoint the Chief Justice upon consent of the National Assembly; other judges are also to be appointed by the President upon the recommendation of the Chief Justice. Of the nine Constitutional Review Committee members who conduct investigations of violations of the Constitution, three are members of the judiciary, three are appointed directly by the President, and the remainder are elected or nominated from among the National Assembly which, in fact, comes under the strong influence of the chief executive. Within these limits, the court takes part in the administrative process by investigating violations of the Constitution and by reviewing the conduct of administrative trials and proceedings.

In some political systems, a vital element in the administrative system consists of local elected officials, who, owing their authority, position and allegiance to local constituencies, contribute to the pluralism of constitutional power, act as counterweights to the central administration, and reduce the decision-costs of the national bureaucracy. In Korea, however, authority has for centuries been centralized vertically as well as horizontally and local officials are to the present day appointed by the government in Seoul. (A partial exception are the Boards of Education which are composed in part of locally elected officials.) It is impossible to gauge fully the consequence for development of this traditional practice. It is possible that the current determinedly achievement-oriented central administration would have had less success in implementing its developmental policy if local interests had been legally organized to intrude and obstruct national decisions. On the other hand, the resolution of local problems might proceed more rapidly if responsibility was closer to home.

Among efforts to involve various non-governmental interests in policy-making and administration, one must include the system of advisory committees, used with varying degrees of success, in all government ministries. The ideology underlying this practice is drawn from popular democratic theory and, more proximately perhaps, from the Jacksonian ideal of public service. As such, it is an alien concept in Korea on the same order as classic parliamentarianism. The fundamental object of this ideal is to further democratic public administration, the belief being that all but the feeble-minded are competent to hold public offices and, in consequence, to further the neutrality, responsibility and public-regardfulness of administration. Advisory committees in the executive agencies were introduced into Korea by the U.S. Military Government immediately after the end of World War II. Advisory committees were organized with apparent randomness under the pretext, or with the hope, of extending democratic administration. It is an undeniable fact, however, that they generated many problems, perhaps more than they alleviated, and the initial objectives of the institution were seriously compromised in action, plagued by the same absurdities of faction, favoritism and instability associated with earlier constitutional systems.

The total number of various administrative committees as of 1962 was 469, of which advisory committees numbered 222. Twenty-nine of these advisory committees were in the Ministry of Finance; 27 in the Ministry of Health and Social Affairs; 25 in the Ministry of Commerce and Industry; 16 in the Ministry of Home Affairs; 15 in the Ministry of Education; 14 in the Ministry of National Defense; 12 in the Ministry of Agriculture and Fisheries; 11 in the Economic Planning Board; 10 in the Ministry of Transportation; and 9 in the Ministry of Communications.[11] Beyond problems of personalities, the majority of these advisory committees involved innumerable organizational problems: for example, many functioned in name only; others overlapped in responsibility or were ambiguous in organizational objective. In order to reduce these defects, the government carried out committee consolidations during 1966-68 and 1970-71. As a result, the number of committees was reduced sharply to 164 by 1975. These are, of course, advisory committees which represent the demands and opinions of various and relevant publics in the policy-making and implementation process, or which perform an important communications function by articulating government policy to their constituents. Still, many of them exist simply to enhance the appearance of a popular administrative structure rather than to perform valuable public functions.

In turning attention to the governmental bureaucracy itself, it should be understood, first, that the bureaucracy of Korea was formed on the foundations of the long autocratic tradition of the Yi Dynasty, which lasted five hundred years. Traditional Korea's governmental structure was characterized by a highly centralized patrimonial bureaucracy backed by Confucian culture. Confucian norms, which remain a vital part of modern Korean culture, emphasized autocratic, vertical human relations, self-effacing authoritarianism, and patriarchism in all sectors and levels of society during the Yi Dynasty.[12] The value premises of the bureaucracy of the Yi Dynasty must be understood in this context. As indicated by Max Weber, it was bureaucracy of a type characterized by administration on behalf of the king's household by the literati, the distribution of government offices according to the arbitrary decision of the king, strict discrimination in the social standing of the people and ruling class, and a generalized tendency to elevate the government vis-a-vis the people.[13] Under this ruling system, it was the mandarins who often exercised pivotal power, and Yi society oscillated between absolute monarchy and rule by the mandarins. The government offices held by the mandarins carried power and prestige, provided income, yielded consumption and enjoyment, and granted opportunities to avoid taxes and conscription.[14]

These latter characteristics prompted, contrary to Confucian ethics, a self-orientation among bureaucrats and consequent neglect of the people. The state examination system, established mainly for the children of the aristocratic class, was the avenue for taking men of high but narrow talent into government office on the basis of merit. The traditional state examination system was adapted to the higher and ordinary civil service examinations during the Japanese colonial rule of Korea and is still in use today.[15] In its current version it has, whatever its limitations, provided Korea with an often able and unusually intelligent higher civil service.

The bureaucracy of the Japanese colonial period provided the central means for extending Japan's rule over Korea. The traditional centralization of power was thus further strengthened to meet the objective of de-Koreanizing the peninsula. High-ranking government offices were occupied exclusively by the Japanese, as pointed out in Chapter 1. The strict and largely successful Japanese control of the Korean people was facilitated by the deeply rooted consciousness of administrative prerogatives and respect for officials traditional in the Land of the Morning Calm. On the other hand, the brutal and discriminatory treatment of the Korean people deepened their antagonism towards the ruling bureaucrats and their imposed and arbitrary system of laws. The autocratic bureaucracy established by the Japanese to maintain control over a foreign population, together with traditional practices, left a legacy of arbitrary bureaucratic tendencies which to some extent still persist.[16]

After Korea attained independence from Japan, the relationship of government and people was formally reversed, that is to say, government was now to be the servant of the people. Notwithstanding administrative reforms instituted several times in recent years and the administrative purification drive, which has been pursued vigorously for years and with major positive results, elements of authoritarianism, nepotism, mannerism, and favoritism still remain in the Korean bureaucracy. Nonetheless, an important contribution to Korean economic development has been made by an increasingly rational and competent bureaucracy. Indeed, performance at the higher levels of the administrative service would seem to compare favorably with that in other modern industrial societies, where, similarly, public rectitude is not always above scrutiny.

The Korean bureaucracy has undergone many trials during the periods of social confusion produced by Liberation, the Korean War, and two major political upheavals. Through crises and natural evolution it has been transformed gradually in its social composition. This can be seen from the emergence of younger senior officials, usually university educated, as well as one-time soldiers, in high administrative positions.[17] Through increased educational levels, better pay, determined political leadership, increased experience in complex and large-scale management, a rigorous entry system predicated on merit, and improved morale, the Korean bureaucracy is moving closer to the classic legal-rational model, while retaining some positive features of the traditional system.

Economic Policy-Making Organs

Public policy-making consists in the making and implementing of choices which are authoritative and binding for a whole society. In Western liberal societies, it seems natural that the powers of administration, legislation and adjudication are related mutually if sometimes antagonistically to that process. As we have noted, such governmental pluralism and division of function are foreign to the Korean political tradition. Moreover, recent regimes have centralized and strengthened administrative power, and the policy-making organs are located largely in the executive branch of government. This has been especially true since the promulgation of the Yushin Constitution, under which most national policies are to be made by the executive with the National Assembly functioning to debate, ratify, or marginally amend the administration's proposals. This political tendency is apparent from the the constitution itself and such facts as that the total number of legislative bills introduced by the executive is overwhelming compared to those originating with Assembly members.[18] (Of course, this latter tendency is a universal one in complex societies.)

Taking this reality into consideration, we will here deal mainly with the economic policy-making organs of the executive, beginning with the Office of the President. Consideration of other important but essentially non-economic policy agencies (e.g., The National Security Council) is not relevant to present concerns.

Office of the President

There is no doubt that the top policy-maker in the Korean government is the President, whose formidable powers under the Yushin Constitution were discussed above. The Office of the President consists of the central and personal staffs which act on the President's behalf. Those who directly assist the President in policy-making are the Special Assistants and Political Secretariats. The former consist of nine special assistants at the ministerial and vice-ministerial level with functional responsibilities for national defense, internal politics, international politics, culture-education, social affairs, economy (1), economy (2), and inspection. They present recommendations which they have developed to the President and provide advice and suggestions as requested by him. The relationship between the President and these special assistants is more personal and informal than with Cabinet ministers. The Political Secretariats are divided into four divisions: the First Political Secretariat deals with politics, political party matters, national defense, foreign affairs, and justice; the Second Political Secretariat deals with home affairs, education, and health and social affairs; the First Economic Secretariat has responsibility for finance, economic planning and other matters related to economic management; and the Second Economic Secretariat handles matters relating to science and technology, defense industry, and heavy and chemical industries. The secretaries comprising the Political Secretariat are public officials seconded from the administrative agencies and play, in effect, the role of a small cabinet. Although there is no formal relation between these secretaries and Special Assistants, it is understood that close functional relations are maintained. The formal duties assigned to the Political Secretariats are to: (1) carry out general analyses of the present state of affairs and assist the President in formulating policies; (2) handle matters of planning and coordination under direct control of the President; (3) perform comprehensive analyses of condition obtaining in each administrative branch; (4) evaluate the performance of each ministry. The Political Secretariats performing these duties serve to link the President directly to each ministry, and their influence in controlling each administrative agency is very significant. The coherence of policy design in Korean development and the effectiveness of policy implementation, a phenomenon commented on by all observers, is in no small part due to the energy, power and presidential access enjoyed by these secretariats.

Cabinet Council

The Cabinet Council of the Korean government differs from cabinets in parliamentary systems in that it is not the top legislative organ; it also differs from the American cabinet system in that it has constitutional status. Thus the Cabinet Council is in the ambiguous position of being neither a legislative nor an advisory organ but a deliberative one.[19] The Cabinet Council is presided over by the President, and the Prime Minister, appointed by the President, assists him as vice-chairman. This Council is composed of between fifteen and twenty-five members appointed by the President upon the recommendation of the Prime Minister. Although the Prime Minister may propose the dismissal of a cabinet member to the President, the President can dismiss cabinet members irrespective of the premier's approval. Matters to be deliberated on by the Cabinet Council are specified in the Constitution, and include: (1) basic planning of national administration and general policy of the government; (2) declaration of war, peace treaties and other important foreign policy issues; (3) basic planning of budget-settlement bills, disposal of national property, contracts and/or agreements which may impose burdens on the state and other important financial matters; (4) delineation of authority among administrative agencies; (5) evaluation and analysis of administrative matters; (6) formulation and coordination of important policies of each administrative branch; and (7) examination of petitions relating to government policies submitted or referred to the government.

The Cabinet Council meets weekly and the presence of the President is rare. In most cases, the Cabinet meeting is presided over by the Prime Minister and the President receives an indirect report from a political secretary who attends the Cabinet meeting as an observer. In practice it has turned out that Cabinet members are often indifferent to matters which are beyond their operational jurisdiction; the Council is forced to attend to an overly-long and varied agenda; and the size of the Council itself has been unwieldly. In such matters it suffers from weaknesses familiar to the American cabinet system. As an instrument for legitimizing policy, however, it serves an important political function.

Economic Ministers' Conference

The importance assigned by the government to economic development and to the successful implementation of the long-range economic development plans has militated for very close coordination and cooperation among those administrative agencies with economic responsibilities. For this purpose, the Economic Ministers' Conference was established as a sub-committee within the Cabinet Council. This Conference is composed of the Ministers of the Economic Planning Board, Foreign Affairs, Finance, Agriculture and Fisheries, Commerce and Industry, Construction, Transportation, Communications, and a Minister without Portfolio in charge of economic affairs. Matters discussed by this Conference include: (1) economic problems which require further deliberation by the Cabinet Council; (2) economic development planning and other national and foreign policies of economic importance; (3) financial investment and monetary plans of the government; (4) coordination problems between and among agencies concerned with finance, banking and prices; and (5) issues referred in accordance with decision of the Cabinet Council. Matters discussed at the Economic Ministers' Conference are introduced to the

Cabinet Council through the Vice-Ministers. Although the Conference may appear to be subordinate to the Council, it functions to coordinate activities of the economic agencies before economic problems are discussed on an overall basis by the Council and is never over-ruled by the Council. As a forum with a rather specific focus, a heavy but integrated agenda and limited size, the Conference performs important communication, educational and management functions.

Vice-Ministers' Conference

The Vice-Ministers' Conference is composed of the vice-minister of each government branch for the deliberation of important policies in advance of the Cabinet Council, and thereby seeks to advance cooperation among the administrative agencies. The Cabinet Council is a constitutional organ while the Vice-Ministers' Conference is a serious working-level and professional one which engages in the preliminary consideration of national policies. It is here that many matters are staffed-out before being considered by the constitutional and political authorities.

Economic-Science Council

This Council was established by statute in 1968 to provide advice and suggestions as requested by the President on policies relating to the development of the national economy and the promotion of science. This Council is presided over by the President and consists of members appointed by the President from among those who have knowledge and experience in economics and science. It also has a secretariat which frames matters to be presented to the Council and organizes data and conducts studies in the fields of economy and science and related areas. It is especially noteworthy that this Council deliberates and examines medium and long-range economic policies and planning for the development of economic and science sectors. It has an important role in the formation and consideration of the five-year development plans.

Office of Planning and Coordination

This organization is under the direct control of the Prime Minister and assists him in reviewing and improving the coordination and capabilities of the administrative agencies. It consists of a director at the vice-ministerial level and, as its name implies, is the major planning and coordination mechanism for all the administrative branches, including the economic agencies. Accordingly, it serves as a pipeline that collects and filters information on the whole of administrative activity. In recent years especially, it has been concerned to detect and prevent maladministration and, most importantly, to analyze and evaluate the effectiveness of policy implementation and overall administration through the Evaluation Professors Group, a group composed of university professors whose relative independence and expertise have made valuable contributions in improving the efficiency and effectiveness of policy planning and implementation.

Government and Ruling Party Joint Meeting

Under the Yushin system, competitive party politics of the sort conventional in Anglo-American and other liberal systems is not present, and the functional contributions of parties to the policy process must be understood differently, at least to some degree. The parties are less instruments of interest aggregation than of policy dissemination and propagation, as well as deliberation and legitimation. In order to tighten cooperation between the government and ruling party with respect to these latter functions, various formal mechanisms are maintained between them. All conflicts of political opinions are adjusted formally through these means.

The first is the government and ruling Democratic Republican Party (DRP) joint meeting, members of which consist of the President, Prime Minister, Cabinet members, Director of the Central Intellignce Agency, Chief Secretary of the President, several chairmen of party committees, DRP leaders in the National Assembly, and three Permanent Committee chairmen of the Yujeong Hoe, composed of those National Assemblymen appointed by the President. The second is the political conference of the DRP and the administration, which includes all Cabinet members, members of the DRP's Party Affairs Committee, Director of the DRP's Policy-Making Research Office, and the executive members of the Yujeong Hoe. The third is the joint meeting for economic issues which is attended by the economic ministers and members of the policy deliberation committee of the ruling party. These policy consultations between the government and the ruling party function with the concerned government minister without portfolio and the policy-making research office of the ruling party as the principal participants. It is conventional for the government to introduce policy issues which reach levels higher than the Vice-Ministers' Conference to relevant party organs for deliberation and information purposes. In this fashion, the party functions as an additional conduit through which public policies are disseminated to a wider elite and, through media coverage, popular audience. In this sense, the party is an important instrument of communications between the government and public.

The Planning Process in Korean Government

National planning consists of complex relations, manifold and often subtle contributions and acts of issue-raising, agenda-setting, decision, implementation and review on the part of many social and political institutions and actors. It has thus been necessary to enumerate the roles of several of the more important actors in the Korean public policy process. Unfortunately, no one is in a position to assign relative weights of influence in policy formation to these particular institutions. Doubtlessly, their individual influence varies over time and with the issues and personalities involved. Having said this, it seems clear that, perhaps more than in many other LDCs, the organization assigned formal responsibility for national planning, namely the Economic Planning Board, exercises an importance consistent with its title. The formal powers of the EPB are considerable and the political support it has enjoyed has enabled the EPB to plan, and to coordinate daily and annual operational decisions with the five-year plans, with unusual consistency and effectiveness. It is difficult, therefore, to exaggerate the contributions of the EPB to Korean development. (Even so, as we shall note, EPB officials themselves tend to assign credit for the developmental surge not to themselves but to the quality and values of the Korean population.)

In broad outline, the Korean five-year planning process places primary responsibility for initiation upon the EPB, particularly its Economic Planning Bureau. Below, the formal planning process itself is described sequentially.

Firstly, the EPB prepares basic guidelines for the proposed development plan and submits it to each executive agency. Secondly, the executive agencies concerned develop planning proposals for their own direct operations and in cooperation with the state-run and private enterprises whose activities fall within the agencies' spheres of concern. Thirdly, when the plans developed by each executive agency are submitted subsequently to the EPB, the EPB modifies and coordinates agency proposals in light of the targets of the emerging development plan. Fourthly, based on the coordination of its own projections with those of the agencies', the EPB prepares a comprehensive draft plan and refers it for further review to the Cabinet Planning Committee and Advisory Committee, respectively, under the direct control of the Prime Minister. Fifthly, after the draft plan is passed through the review of these committees, it is presented to the Economic-Science Council (ESC) for consideration; suggestions of the Council are then reported to the President. Sixthly, the draft plan accepted by the Cabinet Council is submitted to the President for final approval. This process, illustrated graphically, is shown in Chart 5-1.

A point to be noted here, though not indicated in the formal procedure, is that the EPB invites foreign experts to comment on the formulation of the draft plan and consults with them on sectoral plans as well. Finally, and most importantly, the EPB receives professional advice and cooperation from the Korea Development Institute (KDI) on all phases of the plan, macro and sectoral, including policy targets, tactics and timing. KDI was established by statute in 1970 and given a charter to conduct research

Chart 5-1

Planning Flow of Korea's Five-Year Development Plan

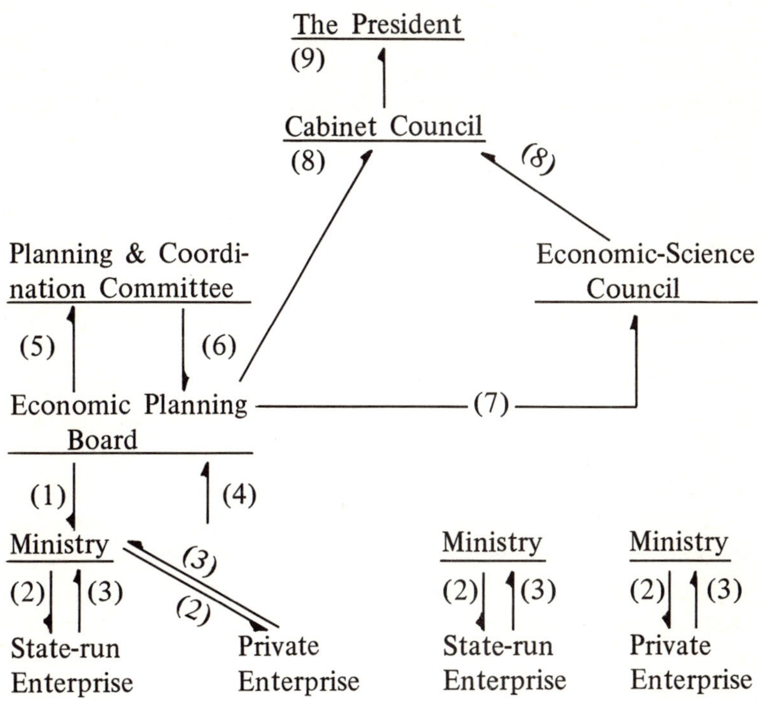

and analysis on a systematic basis on matters relating to the national economy as a whole and to specific problems of particular sectors. With respect to the five-year plans, KDI pursues basic research and makes policy suggestions affecting medium- and long-range forecasting. (Beginning in 1977, KDI will undertake the first fifteen-year planning projections, within which it is hoped subsequent five-year plans can be accommodated.) The size of KDI (over 235 personnel), its quality (including a significant mumber of foreign-educated Ph. D.s), and its already important contributions to the Korean policy process militate for an even larger role in the future.

Administrative Forms, Values and Capability

It is sometimes an intellectually unrewarding and tedious process to inquire very specifically into the formal institutions involved in the policy process of a society, if only because such inquiries may remain entirely at a descriptive and overly particularistic level and include few conclusions of an explanatory or general character. Nonetheless, the atypical success of the Korean development experiences provides reason enough for an institutional description of the planning process, since it is clear that Korean political and administrative institutions and their relationships have figured significantly in that success. Two important conclusions can be drawn from an examination of Korean institutional forms.

First, they have tended formally to conform increasingly to a system of centralized authority, a fact suggested by the above discussion of constitutional changes since the Second World War. We have argued that, in this respect, formal authority in recent years has been organized in a way more or less consistent with traditional patterns and values. Second, notice should be taken of the complexity of the administrative and policy process (common to any complex society, of course), but particularly of the emphasis in Korea on policy coordination and comprehensiveness suggested by the roles of many of the central actors in the process. The Office of the President, the Cabinet Council, the Economic Ministers' Conference, the Vice-Ministers' Conference, state-party organs, the ESC, the EPB, and KDI all have heavy responsibilities to coordinate, integrate and synthesize policy so that a high level of policy comprehensiveness and coherence is achieved.

It is well to reiterate the point made in Chapter 4 that many theorists have recommended against precisely this sort of policy system.[20] Indeed, it is a position that threatens to become intellectual dogma. Of course, no one should pretend that uncertainty, political instability, scarce resources of skill and talent, sunk costs, administrative imperialism and gamesmanship, or individual rather than collective ambition do not constrain comprehensive decision-making. And yet, the Korean experience is one of increasingly sophisticated administrative capabilities, enlarged pools of bureaucratic skills, and persistent attention from the highest levels to a grand strategy of development. There is every reason to be skeptical of claims that Korean development could have proceeded at the pace it has, or even occurred at all, if reliance had been placed on pluralistic bargaining, short time-frames or tentativeness in expressing values to be pursued by public policy. In the Korean case, the centralization of authority and the emphasis on coordination and national planning (even to the point of redundancy)[21] have been consistent with and, on a *prima facie* basis, partly responsible for, accelerated development.

Administration, as Swerdlow points out, is the process of "achieving desired results through organizations."[22] Certainly results have been attained in Korea, as previous chapters have emphasized, but one must still contend with the possibility that the results achieved -- high growth, rapid industrialization, population control, higher living standards -- were not the consequence of administrative and organizational maturation but, rather, of cultural values, rare and fortuitous circumstances, foreign aid, etc. It is argued here, however, without slighting the contributions of Korean culture to development (indeed, culture in our view is the key if any single factor is to be identified) that political stability and a rapidly enlarged administrative capacity have been terribly important. It must be confessed that the very notion of administrative capacity is an ambiguous concept and one scarcely susceptible to acceptable operational definition. To quote Swerdlow again, "The evaluation of [capacity] can have no hard or fast rules, no mechanical procedure for attaining an answer. No check list or cook book can be devised to assess overall administrative capacity and form judgments of what specific policies and actions must be taken to improve macro-administrative capacity."[23]

One can, of course, point to administrative changes which, intuitively if nothing else, must constitute improvements in administrative capacity: experience in managing complex enterprises; higher educational attainments of civil servants; modern statistical and accounting systems; improved staff morale; the diminution of corruption, and so forth. By these standards Korean administrative capacity has been greatly extended over the last decade. By still another test – the achievement of the high goals of successive five-year plans -- the current capacity of the Korean bureaucracy would seem to rank impressively high among the administrative systems of other LDCs.

The Culture of Policy

Political institutions reflect culture, that is, the dominant values, convictions, attitudes and customs of a people. Culture also infuses institutions, provides their dynamism, and affects their informal relationships and processes. For this reason, a mere description of the legal basis of a political order and its policy process will not give a full account of all their relevant dimensions. Culture as a field of study is the major domain of anthropologists and sociologists (among whom the authors are not numbered), and it is fair to say that much remains to be learned about the impact of Korean culture on the policy process. The problem is made more difficult by the fact that culture is not a static backdrop against which society's play enfolds, but is itself a changing element in the historical process. Traditional Korean culture remains a pervasive influence in the policy process, but it must be emphasized that it is people who make culture and that, in an important sense, the Korean people and their culture have been to some undefined degree transformed by the quickening pace of modernization and economic development of the last fifteen years, not to mention the impact of the West and Japan over the last one-hundred years.

Political culture refers to those aspects of the general culture which relate to more or less political things: authority, power, laws, public choices and governmental institutions.[24] Political culture, we have just suggested, changes, but culture is not formed in a day nor does it always change rapidly, for which reason it is useful to inquire into the influence of traditional culture on the Korean policy process.

Hierarchy, or authoritarianism as some would phrase

it, originated in the ancient Confucian ethic which placed a high value on obedience to one's natural superiors, including political authority. The inviolability of hierarchy became the central principle of the five-hundred-year-long Yi Dynasty and found its subsequent expression in the coercive bureaucracy established during the Japanese colonial period. Syngman Rhee's tutelar authoritarianism was also quite within the Korean political tradition, and its eventual arbitrary conduct, to which irresponsible hierarchy degenerates, sustained what had become the ubiquitous and freefloating antagonism of much of the population toward capricious or exploitive rulers. The liberal polity imposed by the U.S. Military Government was as heteronomous in popular perceptions as prior systems had been and even less workable, although the values upon which it was based attracted support from some politically alert and idealistic circles. Partisans of liberal values clashed with the representatives of traditional hierarchical outlooks, producing a bifurcated political culture, a blind opposition to the Rhee regime, and a vicious cycle of cultural clashes made most manifest during the student uprising in 1960.

Personalism, or nepotism in its degenerate form, was also an important element in the Confucian system. Personalism attaches principal importance to patriarchal and less importance to other social relations. The tenacity of the practice is revealed in Korean history, where it has survived for centuries and in the face of innumerable national challenges and incursions. With personalism central in the extended family system (with primogeniture as its foundation), filial devotion was one's prime responsibility; devotion to royalty – or political authority – was of less importance. A sense of mutual interdependence did not penetrate civil society and no reciprocity of confidence developed between the rulers and the ruled. Personal ties were all important and the values of achievement and ability -- extra-family values -- pursued infrequently. Individual advance might very well depend on having met some objective standard (e.g., the civil service examinations), but beyond that such things as family connections, local relations, and academic affiliation were the crucial factors.[26] Thus was produced a tendency to keep outsiders consciously at a distance, resulting in an extremely closed confidentialism. Current efforts to reduce personalism in politics and administration have had considerable success, but much of its force still remains.[27]

In the administrative process, hierarchy is, in the words of Suk-Choon Cho, still to some extent regarded as the "natural form of human relations."[28] Transatlantic norms of equality are alien to many; the superior's role extends not only to the job-related activities of their subordinates but to all aspects of life: family finances, marriages, deaths, births, celebrations. Loyalty and service are the reciprocal values. The dysfunctional consequences for administration are several: cross-organizational coordination is made difficult, at least at lower and middle-levels; criticisms from below are not raised; initiative is suppressed; clients may be treated cavalierly.[29] By the same token, it is possible that the hierarchical emphasis and its corollary, prompt obedience, can on occasion advance the effective implementation of policy. Once a decision is taken, continuing debates which occur in other (e.g., the American) systems do not inhibit the achievement of goals. For a society in a hurry, such as Korea, hierarchy may have its redeeming aspects.

Personalism in administration similarly has functional and dysfunctional aspects from the standpoint of goal achievement. Ascriptive standards rather than expertise may predominate in decisions and do violence to rational administration but, since the factions bound by personalism extend beyond formal task groups, highly efficient if informal lines of communication are available. In the absence of such informal channels, administration might become more formalistic, rule-bound and inert.

Industriousness, closely related to the materialistic and this-worldly orientation of traditional Northeast Asian culture, is apparent in every corner of the social and policy process.[31] Modernization in Korea has meant the harnessing of this extraordinary energy (the "work ethic") to developmental objectives. In the view of many observers, industriousness is the prime traditional orientation which, along with more contingent variables such as sensible policy and political stability, explains much of the Korean success.

It is of course not true that traditional culture remains intact in Korea. Korean society has undergone amazing structural changes in recent years as a consequence of economic growth. A traditional agricultural society has been rapidly urbanized. Seoul alone now contains some 20 per cent of the entire population, and its population density is the highest in the world. The development of transportation and communication networks has produced a "one-day" living sphere for the whole country. Western and Japanese influences and the export-oriented economic structure have introduced to all levels of society new fashions, ideas, aspirations and, inevitably, basic values. What new cultural system will emerge in these circumstances cannot be fully known. Many traditional cultural features will doubtlessly remain to become fused with the cosmopolitan values of world culture.

As concerns the political culture specifically, the role

of leadership is apt to be crucial in shaping the dominent political values which may emerge in tomorrow's Korea. The government of Park Chung Hee seeks to model the Korean polity not on the basis of Western liberal forms, which have never in any case been institutionalized in Korea, but on terms and values which fit the Korean situation. This goal is put forward most authoritatively by the Yushin Reforms of 1972 and in numerous writings and speeches of President Park.[32] Although the operational and structural requirements for Korean democracy have not been fully delineated by the political leadership, the goals include social stability, prosperity, equitable income distribution, self-reliance, mutual cooperation, voluntary participation in community undertakings, and the elimination of administrative irrationalities and corrupt practices. As a trading, and hence necessarily a cosmopolitan nation, it is recognized that Korea must remain an open society, although the precise legal and moral rights and obligations which citizens are to possess vis-a-vis the state are still amorphous and in need of further definition.

Changes in traditional bureaucratic practices are also well-advanced. The government pursues an unceasing anti-corruption policy, punishes malefactors severely, and publishes full details on exposes. Tax evaders, including the rich and powerful, have felt the full weight of administrative and legal sanctions. The status of the specialist in administration has improved -- the specialist having been denigrated in traditional administration in favor of the generalist -- and expertise and experience are increasingly the bases of influence in the policy and implementation process. The vigor with which policy is implemented has improved remarkably with determined support from the highest levels, with improved statistical and accounting systems, and with advanced administrative techniques and better-trained personnel.

One cannot always judge from studies of social background how people are apt to behave in positions of authority, but it is worth noting that, under the Park regime, higher civil servants are younger, better-educated and with greater foreign experience than under previous governments, and more from rural, poor and working-class backgrounds.[33] Many of them owe their achievements to personal effort and talent and not to personal connections or social status. Attitude surveys among higher civil servants show that traditional authoritarian aspects were thought to remain (most thought administrators continue to put "government above the people"), but also that much change has occurred (e.g., most perceived that proposals from subordinates would be welcome and effective). Perceptions of the fairness of personnel administration were largely favorable and an overwhelming majority were reported as satisfied with their jobs (they were less pleased with their incomes). Importantly, most were confident that the goal of economic development could be obtained and that "self-sufficiency" would be achieved within 6-15 years.[34] The positive-orientation of ranking civil servants is itself important to an understanding of Korean development.

It is instructive to record the reaction of two higher level civil servants in the Economic Planning Board when they were asked for their own explanations of Korean economic growth. The same question was raised with other interviewees, numbering some thirty bureau chiefs and section heads, in the EPB and the economic ministries, virtually all of whom replied in the same vein.

> Korean policy is active and timely. Government leadership is most important. We have convinced

> the people to work hard. We are a very, very diligent people. They are all busy. Ask anyone in the street; they will say our future is bright. Also, the EPB is very important. We are fortunate: the DPM [the Deputy Prime Minister who is also the Minister of the EPB] can control all the cabinet members. He has the budget here in the EPB. If it were separate, we could not have good organization. Efficient project implementation attracts additional savings from here and abroad. Once we achieve more success we may separate planning and budgeting, but coordination at this time is best. Our younger staff members are very pragmatic and well-educated.

Policy, institutions, leadership, implementation and education, in this official's view, combine to explain the Korean achievement. Said another:

> Economic common-sense is important, but the Korean emphasis on education is the key. Early expansion in education now represents 15-20 years of accumulated assets. Before, farmers would sell their bull to send sons to university. Everyone, even small-farmers, discusses economic development. We have abundant, quite good labor, easily trained. But simple labor is not now a sufficient weapon. Now we must compete in skilled labor and technologically advanced industry. Now we can compete with Japan and Italy -- in electronics, shipbuilding, industrial machinery. We have an effective administration.

The words are different but the overall thrust much the same. Sound policy, a diligent and able work force, a determination to compete, advance and achieve, and effective organization are identified as important ingredients in economic development.

Summary

Despite a contemporary academic tendency to de-emphasize the importance of political institutions and other political factors in determining levels and patterns of public policy distributions, a strong *prima facie* case can be made that Korean economic development has been in large part due to the consolidation and stabilization of political power and the determination with which policy has been implemented by political leadership and an increasing administrative capacity. With the exception of the brief interlude of the Chang government in the early 1960s, constitutional reforms in Korea have tended to augment the authority of central, and particularly executive, institutions and have moved away from the pluralistic power systems conventional to parliamentary and limited presidential systems. In this, the traditional pattern of political authority has been resurrected but on the basis of a greatly extended bureaucratic capability. Policy is articulated centrally, and integrated through a complex set of planning, reviewing, deliberative and implementing administrative institutions. Powerful authority at the presidential level and strong coordinating executive agencies have provided the government with the means to pursue a large and comprehensive development strategy with remarkable results. The Korean policy system is therefore quite unlike the systems of marginal adjustment and partisan interplay which occupy so much of the policy space in settled industrial democracies.

Political institutions are given dynamism by culture. In Korea, Confucianism continues to influence politics and administration, especially as concerns hierarchy, obedience, personalism, respect for the generalist and personal industriousness. The structural transformation that has occurred in the last fifteen years, however, has given force to new attachments, hopes and beliefs, and it may be said that a new Korean culture is at this time in the process of creation. As part of the general culture, Korean political and administrative culture is in the process of redefinition, with its operational code still unclear, particularly with respect to the role of popular participation and civic rights and obligations. Western liberal values, in the government's view, are appropriate only if they are found to fit Korean requirements and goals. These requirements -- survival and economic development -- and goals -- social stability, equity, community cooperation and self-help -- will continue to be defined internally.

Changes in the traditional administrative culture have been in the direction of the legal-rational system and more able civil servants have been recruited to staff a government that faces the increasingly difficult and sophisticated task of organizing, directing and stimulating a new and complex industrial society.

Notes

1. For example, see David Easton's, *A Framework for Political Analysis* (Englewood Cliffs, N.J.: Prentice-Hall, 1965), p. 49, and *A Systems Analysis of Political Life* (New York: Wiley, 1965), p. 214.

2. The basic argument may be found in Thomas R. Dye's, *Understanding Public Policy* (Englewood Cliffs, N.J.: Prentice–Hall, 1972), Chapter 12, and *Politics, Economics and the Public: Policy Outcomes in the American States* (Chicago: Rand McNally, 1966). Replies to Dye's thesis that politics is subservient to economics in influencing policy outcomes include John A. Fenton, *People and Parties in Politics* (Glenview, Ill.: Scott, Foresman, 1966), and a partial refutation by Ira Sharkansky and Richard I. Hofferbert, "Dimensions of State Politics, Economics and Public Policy," *American Political Science Review*, Vol. 63 (September, 1969), pp. 867-79.

3. E. g., Phillips Cutright, "Political Structure, Economic Development, and National Social Security Programs," *The American Journal of Sociology*, Vol. 70 (March, 1965), pp. 537-50.

4. See Alexander J. Groth, *Comparative Politics: A Distributive Approach* (New York: Macmillan, 1971).

5. Irving Swerdlow, *The Public Administration of Economic Development* (New York: Praeger, 1975), pp. 212. A useful approach to institutional analysis is Milton J. Esman and Hans C. Blaise, "Institution Building Research -- The Guiding Concepts," University of Pittsburgh, Inter-University Research Program in Institution Building, GSPIA, 1966.

6. Hong-Joo Moon, *The Korean Constitution* (Seoul: Hyun Am Sa, 1975), p. 328. This, and the following citations with Korean places of publication, refer to Korean-language sources and are translated here for the convenience of English-language readers. The Romanization of Korean names conforms to the style of the *Korean Public Administration Review*.

7. The fourth revision of the Constitution occurred in November, 1960 under the Democratic Party and established authority for the retroactive punishment of anti-democratic activities. As such, it did not involve governmental organization or the distribution of legal powers.

8. Tae-Hyun Han, *The Constitution* (Seoul: Bup Moon Sa, 1973), p. 45.

9. The sixth revision of the Constitution was adopted by referendum on October 17, 1969. As this revision altered the clause forbidding the election of a president beyond two terms, there was no immediate change

in the power structure itself, although the impact obviously was to further strengthen the executive.

10. It has been argued that the role of the Cabinet Council and the Prime Minister in the Fourth Republic is to check any arbitrary decisions of the President. See Woon-Tai Kim, *et al., Korean Politics* (Seoul: Bak Yung Sa, 1976), p. 298.

11. Sai-Duk Oh, "Problems and Reform Measures of Administrative Committees in Korea", *Kyung Hee Law Journal* (1975), p. 134.

12. Tae-Lim Yoon, *Personality Types of the Korean People* (Seoul: Modern Education Publishing Co., 1964), pp. 207-244.

13. Max Weber's description of Confucian bureaucracy is particularly apt. See the translation by Talcott Parsons and A.M. Henderson, *The Theory of Social and Economic Organization* (New York: The Free Press, 1947), pp. 345-355.

14. See Woon-Tai Kim, "The Historical Study of Public Administration in the Yi Dynasty," *Korean Journal of Public Administration,* Vol. 6 (1967), p. 35; and Dong-Suh Bark, *The Historical Development of Korean Bureaucracy* (Seoul: Institute of Korean Studies, 1961), pp. 43-57.

15. See Hahn-Been Lee, "Political Changes and Bureaucratic Development Since Korean Liberation," *Korean Journal of Public Administration,* Vol. V (1967), p. 2; and Suk-Choon Cho, *Theory of Organization* (Seoul: Bup Moon Sa, 1973), p. 76.

16. Hahn-Been Lee, "Political Changes and Bureaucratic Development Since Korean Liberation," p. 5.

17. *Ibid.*, pp. 5-23. Also see Woon-Tai Kim, "A Study of Korean Higher Civil Servants and Some Proposals for Reforming the Bureaucratic System," *Korean Journal of Public Administration,* Vol. 4 (1966), pp. 243-265.

18. Dong-Suh Bark, "Policy-Making in the Korean Executive Branch," *Korean Journal of Public Administration,* Vol. 4 (1966), pp. 207-15.

19. It has been contended that the Cabinet Council is the supreme organ for national policy-making. See Wan-Kee Baik, "The Korean Administrative Process," in Woo-Tai Kim (ed.), *Korean Politics,* p. 410.

20. For example, Charles E. Lindblom, *The Policy-Making Process* (New York: Prentice-Hall, 1968); W. Stolper, *Limitations of Comprehensive Planning in the Face of Comprehensive Uncertainty: Crisis of Planning or Crisis of Planners,* Center for Research on Economic Development, University of

Michigan, Oct. 1969, Discussion Paper No. 10; and, as discussed in Chapter 4, Caiden and Wildavsky, *Planning and Budgeting in Poor Countries* (New York: Wiley, 1974).

21. On the virtues of redundancy, see Martin Landau, "Redundancy, Rationality and the Problem of Duplication and Overlap," *Public Administration Review,* Vol. 29 (1969), pp. 346-58.

22. *The Public Administration of Development,* p. 356.

23. *Ibid.,* p. 359.

24. Useful discussions of the attitudes and backgrounds of Korean policy makers and administrators include Chun-Ju Yoon, *An Introduction to the Korean Political System* (Seoul: Korea University Press, 1961); Tae-Lim Yoon, *The Personality Types of the Korean People;* Hahn-Been Lee, *Social Change and Administration* (Seoul: Bak Young Sa, 1968), Part III; Woon-Tai Kim, *Korean Politics,* pp. 123-203; Moon-Ok Bark, *Korean Government* (Seoul: Bak Young Sa, 1963), pp. 31-46; Moon-Ha Kim, *Korean Political Parties* (Seoul: Ilshin Sa, 1976), pp. 70-108; Suk-Choon Cho, "The Bureaucracy," in Edward R. Wright (ed.), *Korean Politics in Transition* (Seattle: University of Washington Press, 1976); Kyu-Taik Kim and Bae-Ho Hahn, "Korean Political Leaders (1953-1962): Their Social Origins and Skills," *Asia Survey,* Vol. 3 (July, 1963); Dong-Suh Bark, "Development Policy Formulation and the Role of Higher Civil Servants," *Korean Journal of Public Administration,* Vol. 9 (1970), pp. 8-25; Hoon Yu, "The Social Background of Korean Higher Civil Servants," *Ibid.,* Vol. 4 (1966), pp. 243-265.

25. Woon-Tai Kim, *Korean Politics,* pp. 125-36.

26. Tae-Lim Yoon, *The Personality Types of the Korean People,* pp. 207-280.

27. See Moon-Ha Kim, *Political Parties in Korea,* pp. 156-161; and Suk-Choon Cho, "The Bureaucracy," pp. 76-77.

28. Suk-Choon Cho, "The Bureaucracy," p. 74.

29. *Ibid.,* p. 75.

30. *Ibid.,* p. 77.

31. Korean writers on development sometimes fail to give sufficient attention to the Korean work ethic, although it is commented on by all foreign visitors and public officials are well aware of its importance.

32. See Chung-Hee Park's, *The State, The Revolution and I* (Seoul: Hyang Moon Sa, 1963); *The Path of Our Nation* (Seoul: Tong-A Publishing Co., 1962); *The Collected Speeches of President Park* (Seoul: Tong-A Publishing Co., 1973).

33. See Notes 17 and 18 for references, and In-Jung Whang, *Elites and Economic Programs: A Study of Changing Leadership for Economic Development in Korea,* 1955-67 (Ph.D. Thesis: University of Pittsburgh, 1967).

34. See Notes 17, 18 and 33.

Chapter 6

Conclusion

The social conditions that obtained in Korea in the first half of this century, and the policy directions pursued by the Korean government in the economic sphere over the last ten to fifteen years, have been discussed in earlier chapters. The desperate economic circumstances in which Korea found itself after the Second World War and a half-century of colonial exploitation were compounded by the appalling devastation to life and property wrought by the Korean War. In 1953, Korea was an extremely poor country in every sense of the term: it was over-populated, productivity was low, subsistence living standards prevailed, natural resources were meager, the economy was primarily agricultural, and illiteracy was still high; moreover, savings and investment were low, foreign trade was nil, a comprehensive developmental strategy had not been formed, public institutions were arbitrary, inchoate, inexperienced, and both elite and popular morale was demoralized and often cynical. Few countries in the world offered fewer ostensible prospects for broad, rapid and prolonged economic development.

And yet, by the late 1960s and into the 1970s, Korea had emerged as perhaps the most successful of all developing countries in transforming and modernizing its economy. Korea is now an industrialized developing country: by the late 1980s, it may well be a modest exporter of capital, will have become a serious middle-sized economic power, and, sometime in the 1990s, should enter the ranks of the developed countries. If the deepening and expansion of the Korean economy continues, even at a rate rather below what circumstances would now seem to warrant, Korea will be the first country in the so-called Third World to have achieved broad, accelerated, self-sustained economic modernization. As an example of what is possible for others, its achievement is of historic importance.

It is not possible to state quantitatively – to weight the variables – how and why this transformation, the so-called "Miracle on the Han," occurred. It has been observed in the text, however, that a comparison of Korea with other LDCs on a whole range of developmental indicators showed Korea's performance in savings and investment, capital efficiency, manufacturing, exports, education, and population control to be consistently among the world's best. Korean development has been widely based, affecting all economic and social sectors.

Policies pursued, including the profitability criterion in state enterprises as a general objective, realistic interest rates and currency valuations, direct government investment in social and physical overhead, assistance to export-oriented industries, inducement of foreign savings, the rationalization of agriculture, and population control have proved remarkably effective in promoting economic development. Flexibility and economic "common sense" rather than rigidity and dogma have characterized the evolution of economic policy. The shifting goals and emphases of the five-year plans have, with some fitful starts in the early 1960s, been rationally selected in light of domestic problems and capabilities and the international economic environment. Earlier planning goals sought to expand certain key industries, to increase agricultural output and to develop import-substitution industries, while the next phase focused on improvements in the industrial structure, the expansion of exports and improved agricultural incomes. By the early 1970s, it became possible to direct development toward heavy and chemical industries, self-sufficiency in food grains and improvements in the balance of payments. The overriding objective throughout has been a rapid and sustained increase in per capita GNP.

If the ambitious goals of the Fourth Five-Year Plan (1977-81) had been stipulated in the early 1960s, they would surely have been viewed as hopelessly utopian. The fact that they now seem altogether reasonable and attainable is testimony to the extraordinary character of Korean development. The Fourth Plan calls, for the first time, for improvements in social welfare, for continued growth, and for heightened efficiency in order to compete internationally in heavy and chemical industries. Under the Fourth Plan, the economy is expected to grow at an annual rate of 9.2 per cent; per capita GNP is to reach $1,512 in current prices by 1981; exports are to grow by 16 per cent annually and to be valued at $20 billion in current prices in 1981; population growth will remain low. In Table 6-1, the plan's projections of economic activity over the 1977-81 period are summarized.

Policies to be pursued in key sectors include, in the pricing area, reduction in the money supply to less than 20 per cent (which should reduce inflation and increase savings), a reduction in subsidies to industry, the readjustment of utility charges to opportunity cost levels, and the streamlining of marketing structures (all of which should increase efficiency). In the fiscal area, a further devolution of state enterprises to private ownership is contemplated

	Unit	1975(A)	1976	1977	1978	1979	1980	1981(B)	Increase (B/A)
Gross National Product	in bil. won at 1975 constant prices	9,080.3	10,442.4	11,486.6	12,520.4	13,647.3	14,875.5	16,214.3	1.8 times
	in $1 mil. at current prices	18,761	24,811	30,852	36,966	43,141	50,312	58,660	–
Economic Growth Rate	%	8.3	15.0	10.0	9.0	9.0	9.0	9.0	–
GNP Deflator	1975=100 %	100.0	115.0	130.0	142.9	153.0	163.7	175.1	–
Total Population	in 1,000 persons	35,381	35,860	36,436	37.019	37.605	38,197	38,807	1.1
(Growth Rate)	%	(–)	(1.64)	(1.60)	(1.58)	(1.58)	(1.60)	(1.62)	–
Per Capita GNP	in dollars at current prices	532	692	847	999	1,147	1,317	1,512	–
Growth Rates:									
Agriculture, Forestry, Fisheries	%	7.1	7.0	4.0	4.0	4.0	4.0	4.0	
Mining, Manufacturing	%	12.9	26.7	17.2	14.1	13.6	13.2	12.8	
Social Overhead Capital, Others	%	5.8	11.8	7.9	7.5	7.5	7.6	7.6	
Consumption (Expenditure)	in bil. won at 1975 prices	7,444.4	8,247.7	8,954.5	9,646.4	10,368.8	11,146.0	11,983.3	1.6
Capital Investment	"	2,478.4	2,896.5	3,097.9	3,294.6	3,540.4	3,855.3	4,219.9	1.7
(Investment Rate)	%	(27.3)	(27.7)	(27.0	(26.3)	(25.9)	(25.9)	(26.0)	
Domestic Savings	in bil. won at 1975 prices	1,635.9	2,194.7	2.532.1	2,874.0	3,278.5	3,729.5	4,231.0	2.6
(Savings Rate)	%	(18.0)	(21.0)	(22.0)	(23.0)	(24.0)	(25.1)	(26.1)	
Overseas Savings	in bil. won at 1975 prices	1,023.0	701.8	565.8	420.6	261.9	125.8	11.1	
(Savings Rate)	%	(11.3)	(6.7)	(5.0	(3.4)	(1.9)	(0.8)	(0.1)	
Exports	in $1 mil. at 1975 prices	5,003	6,750	8,248	9,692	11,194	12,705	14,165	2
Imports	"	6,674	7,841	9,023	10,157	11,343	12,563	13,826	1.8

SOURCE: Economic Planning Board, December, 1976.

(reducing corruption and lowering decision-costs), public employees are to receive substantial salary increases, customs duties are to be reduced (lowering consumer prices and encouraging greater efficiency among producers for the domestic market), and tax advantages to savers are to be increased. Expansions in housing, technical education, public transportation, pensions and medical care are to be directed at the enhancement of social welfare, which is one of the major goals of the plan.

There is no evidence that income inequality has heightened during these years of rapid growth, and Korea continues to rank high among the world's nations in equality of income distribution. As Korea reaches higher levels of economic development, its position in international trade will necessarily be altered. Demands are already being heard from the developed market economies in North America and Europe for further liberalization of Korean import policy and for closer policing of Korean export practices. The Fourth Plan seeks to move Korean technology and industrial scale to internationally competitive levels because of such pressures as well as improvements in the balance of payments. While some domestic producers will suffer under such changes, the welfare of Korean consumers will be enhanced.

Broadly intelligent and far-sighted economic planning, in the view of some academic political economists, is not really possible – the reasons are discussed in Chapter 4 and need not be reiterated here. If this is true for most LDCs, it is not true for Korea, where sophisticated economic plans and effective policy implementation have been developed and practiced for nearly twenty years. In this respect, as in its economic performance, Korea appears to be a deviant case among the LDCs. Strong central political institutions, determined executive leadership, and multiple systems of coordination and policy adjustment have led in the process of development. Political stability has made a vital contribution by providing an environment in which increasingly able specialists and managers could act confidently in initiating and implementing the hard decisions which development requires.

The conceptual elegance of a development plan, reliable support from political authority, the skills of administrators, however, will not alone launch or achieve development. Something more subtle is involved as well, namely, the existence or creation of cultural values and aspirations among the masses of people which encourage individuals to work, save, invest, take risks, improve their skills, look to the future, remain hopeful, and act cooperatively. In this respect, the aid of cultural historians, anthropologists and sociologists is indispensable to a better understanding of Korean modernization, and one looks forward to the intellectual contributions that they will surely make as interest in Korean development increases as it must. Culture, policy, institutions and leadership are the keys to development, and form a seamless web to be comprehended in its totality if development is to be understood. Korean development is important in its own right, as its beneficiaries will be quick to acknowledge, but it is important as well in giving proof to the proposition that history is made by people, that life need not be accepted fatalistically, and that rapid, sustained and broad improvements in material welfare can be accomplished in the face of the most unpromising circumstances.

Korea continues to face many problems: its national security is under constant threat from an unremittingly hostile and aggression-prone regime to the north; many people are still poor; administrative discretion is not always prudently or fairly applied; the international economic system is less one to be managed than endured; voluntary and cooperative public action, while increasing, is still to produce a civic consciousness which would relieve the government of some of its administrative burden; nepotism and corruption, while much reduced and severely punished, continue to be practiced on some occasions; civil rights and obligations require further protection and definition. Many of these, however, are problems that all or most societies face, and it is of course foolish to expect that all social or political problems can be solved permanently in any society. On the other hand, a Korea that is increasingly prosperous, stable, urbanized, industrialized, and highly educated will be well-positioned to ameliorate the worst of continuing abuses and to provide a better life for this and subsequent generations.

We would like to close this volume on a hortatory note. Much of the literature published in the West on political and economic development has tended to yield or reinforce what are generally pessimistic conclusions about the prospects for rapid modernization in the Third World. These pessimistic views are based on many and varied considerations, but especially: (1) analyses of the central tendencies of development patterns around the world; (2) generalized conclusions based on experiences of particular countries which have failed in their development objectives. With such scholarly foci, optimism concerning the prospects for development is scarcely warranted. There has also emerged in the literature a new view, based on the presumed failure of developmental efforts, that development must now be understood not to include rapid and sustained improvements in material welfare (that being impossible, or so it is thought) but as cultural and ideological development, in which traditional values are revitalized and the non-material, humane, community values which give vitality and significance to life are stimulated and shared. There is much to be said for the view that economic welfare is not the sum of existence and that a meaningful life does not require material affluence. The view taken here, however, is that it is not necessary to choose between material and cultural development. Poverty, for most people, is not a wholesome state, and only in a society of relative abundance are individuals free to develop fully their talents, ambitions, and higher sensibilities.

Since the Korean case demonstrates that rapid economic development is possible, it would seem worthwhile for developmentalists to examine the Korean case in considerably greater depth, as well as the few other Third World countries that are now well on their way to the founding of advanced economies. A focus on deviant cases is not usually recommended in the social sciences, and for very good reasons if the interest is in general comprehension of the patterns underlying complex phenomena. Developmentalists, however, are normally concerned with the policy implications of their investigations: their task is not so much to understand central tendencies as the conditions of success. It consequently makes eminent sense to consider the uncommon, successful cases, and to discern, if possible, those factors of resources, culture, institutions, policy, and performance that set them apart from the typical cases. For these altogether practical reasons, a greater scholarly attention to the successful examples in the developing world would be a commendable development in itself. If the ingredients of success were known and understood more precisely, policy-makers around the world could conduct their activities with both greater conviction and effect.

A Hypothetical Note

Throughout this volume, we have indicated that Korea's success in mobilizing and extending its resources, that is, in economic development, must be explained by a complex interplay of many variables, including Korean culture (both traditional and evolving), intelligent policy choices, a growing administrative capability, and political stability. Other factors have also been mentioned, such as the international economic and political environment, the trade policies of other countries and, of course, the overall contextual setting of Korea in terms of natural resource endowment, geographical position, population, and so forth.

Ideally, we should like to know precisely how these and perhaps other independent variables interact to affect the dependent variable of economic growth. There are several reasons, however, why their interaction cannot be understood completely at this or perhaps any other time. First, the variables themselves are so "large," that is, encompass so many complex phenomena, that to operationalize them on the basis of current theorizing and data would serve only to obscure and even trivialize the significance of what we wish to convey. What was pointed out in Chapter 5 with respect to administrative capacity – no "check list or cook book can be devised to assess overall administrative capacity" – is equally true of other complex factors which one reasonably believes are or have been important in launching and sustaining Korean development. One could, of course, force these variables into a Procrustean bed which would permit precise measurement. Political stability might, for example, be defined arbitrarily as an absence of civil strife for some period of time, or as the preservation of a constitutional system, or as the persistence in power of some political elite, or as some combination of these or other factors. For some research, it might well be useful to adopt such definitions. In understanding a special case, however, such efforts are apt to produce a limited and superficial, even misleading, understanding of what one seeks to communicate. In the social sciences, the scholar must still often rely on ordinary language and conventional understandings to advance his ideas. Political stability in such usage embodies complicated meanings, including, in addition to the above, some degree of social consensus, elite durability, popular expectations of continuity in policy, confidence of foreign investors and governments, and so forth.

Second, even if the exceedingly complex independent variables considered in this book could be operationalized successfully, the problem of measuring their relative impact on economic development would remain. Theories as to how such factors are interrelated remain inconclusive in spite of the ingenious labors of many social scientists. Just as importantly, the data that would be necessary to give content to a plausible model of development are not entirely available in most societies, either because of the sensitivity of some of the issues involved, financial considerations, the lack of trained researchers, or skepticism towards the models that would guide data-collection activities.

What the scholar would like to be able to do in explaining Korean development is to construct a causal theory, the logical requirements of which are well-enough known. That logic may be illustrated by a brief and largely hypothetic discussion of path analysis applied to the Korean case. Path analysis is a causal model for understanding relationship among variables. It assumes that the values of one variable are caused by the values of another. Path analysis aims at a closed system of analysis. If variable X, the independent variable (say administrative capacity), is presumed to affect Z, the dependent variable (say Korean economic growth), we could, with appropriate operational definitions and measurements of these variables, discover the standardized regression coefficient (the "path coefficient") describing the strength of the empirical relationship between X and Z.

We suspect, however, that X will not "explain" all of the variance in Z. The "unexplained" variance can be computed and treated as a residual that combines all the remaining independent variables. As additional variables are broken out of the residual, the logic of the causal model we seek to develop becomes clearer. If independent variable Y (say policy choices) is added, X may be held constant to determine the independent impact of policy choices on development, or of Y on Z. The value of the residual variable may be consequently reduced and more of the variance in Z explained. However, it is possible that X and Y, while operating directly on Z, are also mediated to some extent through another intervening variable, I (say Korean culture).

This more complex situation can be managed conceptually by path analysis. First, both X and Y are believed to affect I, and this can be represented with appropriate path coefficients. Since I is presumed to affect Z, a path coefficient for that relationship can be given as well. Additional independent variables could further reduce the variance on Z and, as the system closes, the relative weights of the independent variables in influencing Korean development established.

Since the independent variables have not been operationalized in this book, no such causal model of Korean development can be presented here. The following should be understood as a purely illustrative exercise for that reason.

Figure 6–1. Hypothetical Causal Model of Korean Development

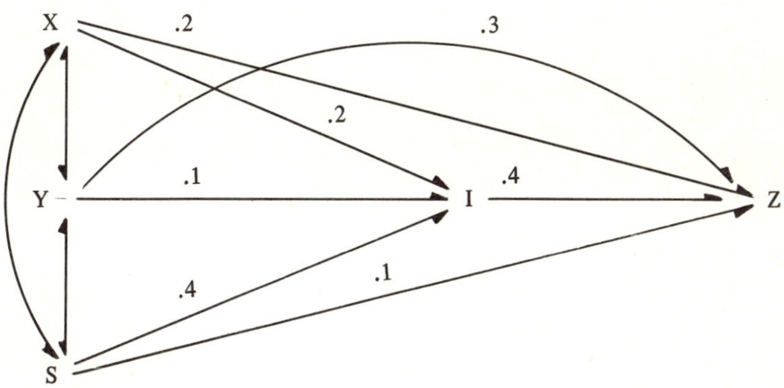

Z = Korean economic development
X = Administrative capacity
Y = Policy choices
I = Korean culture
S = Political stability
Note: coefficients are hypothetical

In Figure 6-1, the two-headed arrows indicate that the independent variables are themselves related (as we would expect these particular variables to be) but that our model does not imply any causal direction. For the one-headed arrows, or paths, we should like to be able to assign path coefficients, and, since Figure 6-1 cannot really be interpreted in their absence, we have taken the liberty of inserting some entirely arbitrary coefficients for illustrative purposes.

The hypothetical path coefficients in Figure 6-1 show that the strongest predictor of Korean development (Z) is Korean culture (I). Looking further into the diagram, we note a strong partial relationship between political stability (S) and Korean culture (I) and a rather weak relationship between political stability (S) and economic development (Z). This suggests that political stability primarily affects Z through the intervening variable. Policy choices (Y), on the other hand, act more directly on Z and less through the intervening variable, while administrative capacity (X) affects Z equally directly and indirectly. In this example, all the variance in Z has been explained, but this is most unlikely to occur in actual fact.

The logic of path analysis is suggested as a general guide to further research on development, although the precision which the method sometimes provides is not possible with respect to many research themes. The pursuit of such precision remains a commendable goal in any case.

Index

About the Authors

L. L. WADE (Ph. D., The University of Oregon) is currently Professor of Political Science at the University of California, Davis, and taught previously at Purdue University and the University of North Carolina, Charlotte. He has been a National Science Foundation Fellow at the London School of Economics and Political Science, a Senior Fulbright Lecturer (Japan) and Researcher (Korea), and has published widely in the fields of public policy analysis and political economy.

BONG-SIK KIM was educated in the United States, where he took his B.S. (Lewis and Clark) and M.A. (University of Oregon) degrees, and Korea (Ph.D., Kyung Hee University). He is currently Professor of Public Administration at Kyung Hee University and, in addition to other publications, is the author of the standard work on the theory and practice of Korean national planning.

Related Titles
Published by
Praeger Special Studies

FUTURE OF THE KOREAN PENINSULA
edited by Young C. Kim
Abraham M. Halpern

NORTH KOREA'S FOREIGN RELATIONS: The Politics of Accommodation, 1945–75
Wayne S. Kiyosaki

COMMUNIST POLITICS IN NORTH KOREA
Ilpyong J. Kim

THE COMMERCIAL FUTURE OF HONG KONG: A Political and Economic Assessment
William F. Beazer

ECONOMIC DEVELOPMENT OF SOCIALIST VIETNAM: 1955–80
Nguyen Tien Hung